Table of Contents

ART OF MAKING KOSHER WINE

Complete Guide for making kosher wine at home

2nd Edition

BARRY NADEL

Dedication

This book is dedicated to the loving

the memory of my father, Sir Daniel Nadel

Chevalier Of the French Legion of Honor.

Rabbi Hanina Ben Dosa said:

Anyone who is liked by his fellow man is liked by God.

Agrosearch

HaSilo St. 9

Kfar Pines, Israel 37920

Publisher's Cataloging-in-Publication data

Nadel, Barry.

A title of a book: Art of Kosher Wine Making / Barry Nadel

ISBN: 9798227548702

1. The main category of the book —Wine —

2. Do it Yourself

Second Edition

INTRODUCTION

Nothing prevents any *Shomer Shabbat* Jew from making the best wines in the world and being kosher.

Winemaking has become a serious hobby in many homes worldwide. There is a long tradition of making kosher wine at home, stretching back many generations. Since wine plays an important role in Jewish rituals, no Jewish community can exist without it. One of the most Jewish symbols is a man holding a cup of wine and making Kiddush. Wine is the only drink that requires a specific blessing (*boreh pri hagafen*).

The function of wine in Jewish tradition inspires and comforts us. Wine lends significance and dignity to a function. Blessing the wine elevates simple occasions to a higher spiritual plane.

The blessing over the cup of wine on Friday nights (*Kiddush*) symbolizes ushering in the holy Sabbath after candle lighting. Wine is also the *central ingredient of the Havdalah service*, separating the Shabbat and holidays from the rest of the mundane week.

When a large enough quorum of men has eaten together (ten), a cup of wine and its attendant blessing concludes the grace after meals. The required drinking of the four cups of wine at the *Pesach Seder* serves as the central point of that holy occasion. These examples demonstrate the critical aspect of wine in Jewish ritual life.

It is no coincidence that one of the seven species of the Land of Israel is the grape. The Torah does not refer directly to grapes (*anavim*) but calls them wine (gefen). Archeologists have found numerous ancient winemaking vats (*gat*) throughout the Land of Israel. They are a feature of every ancient Jewish settlement, testifying to the importance of winemaking to our religion.

Art of Kosher Winemaking

The secrets of home winemaking are divided into two categories. The first and more critical of the two concerns the physical properties of the wine. One needs to produce technically sound wine. I define technically sound wine as clear wine with good color and no off-tastes or odors. The second secret is the blending of varieties. This is all a matter of palate. Similarly, you can alter wine color by adding a small amount of wine from a teinturier variety—varieties with very intense red color—you can make your wine more complex by blending different varieties.

This book is unique for two reasons: First, the approach to home winemaking in this book is to help winemakers produce technologically sound wines. You can make good wine or bad wine from good grapes. Most problems involve adjusting the process to create a clear wine free of off-tastes and smells. Secondly, it provides a step-by-step method of how to produce different types of wine at home.

Winemaking has become a serious hobby in many homes worldwide, but there are many misconceptions about it for those who want to take up the hobby.

Homemade wines are of a low quality.

> This is not true. As with any hobby, the more you practice, the better you become at accomplishing good results. Don't expect great results the first time. However, following the steps in this book, you can make a decent wine the first time.

Wine is time-consuming.

> Isn't that why we want hobbies—to take up our time? Only the beginning is time-consuming: harvesting, cleaning, crushing, and initiating the fermentation. Today, many kits are available that reduce the time needed for the hobby.

Home Wine Making is Expensive.

This was true in the past if you wanted to make any amount of wine beyond 35 liters. Reasonable equipment costs, but unlike other hobbies, the materials are disposable; wine equipment can be used for decades.

Homemade wine spoils easily.

One of the objectives of this book is to teach the winemaker how to prevent his homemade wine from spoiling. This complaint is mainly caused by sloppy procedures. Proper sanitation, especially for your storage vessels, is essential. If you maintain reasonable procedures, the quality of your wine should be maintained for years.

Wine can be simple or complex, and as one's skills in winemaking improve, making a good wine becomes an art form. The winemaker's canvas is his bottle, and his subject is color, aroma, and taste. Producing a technically sound wine is one of the most essential parts of making an excellent complex wine. Technically sound wine will have a clear color, no strange foreign odors, and no off-tastes. Numerous books have been published about wine, each informative on one or more of the many diverse aspects surrounding wine and its processes. This book intends to introduce the general Jewish public to the world of wine and provide specific practical information on how to make and enjoy homemade grape and fruit wines that are technically sound.

There are many books available on home winemaking. Most of them are full of beautiful pictures, sketches, and receipts on how to make wine. This book's intention is not just to teach the how but the why. It intends to inform the public about distinguishing between poor and superior wines by their specific attributes (flavor, aroma, color, bouquet, and taste).

There are many types and styles of wine. Wine experts will inform us that this wine is better than that one or that the aroma and taste of wine X, produced by company A, is superior to wine Y, produced by company B. This booklet will teach one how to sift through the information that is objective and subjective. One critical fact one should never forget is that taste, as opposed to all the other attributes of wine, is one hundred percent subjective. Each individual has his or her likes and dislikes. When it comes to taste, do not depend on anyone else. Your tongue is the best judge of the matter. No matter how many experts tell you the wine is terrible or not technically sound, it's good if you like it.

Wine can be divided into many different categories. Below is a simple system that is easy to follow. For our purposes, grape wines can be divided into three general groups: natural, dessert, and appetizer wines. Below is a table categorizing the different wine types.

Wine Classification

Natural Wines

9-14% Alcohol

A-Still Wines (No excess CO2)

1-Dry Table Wines

No Noticeable Sweetness

a-White

b-Rosé

c-Red

In general, these wines are consumed with food.

B-Slightly Sweet Table Wines

Dessert & Appetizers

15-21% Alcohol

A-Sweet Wines

1-White Muscatel & White Port

2-Red Muscatel & Red Port

B-Sherries (White sweet or dry wines that have been purposely oxidized)

1-Baked

2-Aged

3-Flor

C-Sweet Table Wines

C-Flavored Specialty Wines

1-White

1-Vermouth

2-Red

3-'Old Wines' With Added Caramel

D-Slightly Gassy Wines

1-White

2-Red

E-Sparkling Wines (With large amounts of CO_2)

1-Champagne
(Natural & Bulk)

a-White

b-Pink

2-Artificially
Introduced CO_2

3-Red   Sparkling
Burgundy

.

Natural wines are wines whose alcohol content is made one hundred percent by the natural fermentation of grape sugar into alcohol by yeast. The alcohol and sugar content of these wines depend on how complete the fermentation occurs. Wines of this type are consumed at meals or light foods such as dry white wines with apples and cheese. In Israel, most sweet wine is produced specifically for religious consumption, i.e., *Kiddush* and *Havdalah*. There are also old wines. These are sweet wines with caramel added to them to give them a slightly musty taste and flavor, not at all imitating a truly aged wine.

Appetizer wines are drunk before meals as a prelude to the food. These wines have a slight amount of sweetness. They are wines drunk in the company of other people in small amounts while talking before a meal. Dessert wines also have a high alcohol content (15-21 %). They are consumed after meals or with your dessert. They are consumed in small quantities.

Sparkling wines give off a continual flow of bubbles (CO_2 gas) for an extended period (hours) after opening. Since natural champagnes are expensive, they are associated with joyous occasions today. Authentic sparkling wines are produced by secondary yeast fermentation in a closed container (e.g., a bottle or large vessel). Thus, the CO_2 gas produced by the fermentation is trapped inside the wine and released upon exposure to air.

II. BIOLOGY OF GRAPES AND WINE.

The biology of winemaking involves:

1) Grapes,

2) Yeast, wild and domestic, and

3) Bacteria.

In the past, most kosher wines were made from the European species *Vitis vinifera*. Today, over 5,000 different cultivated varieties are grown around the world. The variety of grapes used for winemaking will determine the wine's color, aroma, acid content, and flavor.

Grapes

Grapes are long-lived woody bushes, some over a 100 years old. Their growing season is from spring to fall, and they produce fruit in clumps called clusters or bunches. The quality of grapes of any variety depends on their genetic makeup, environmental conditions in which they grew, accumulative heat, wind, water supply, disease, and insects, and the care the plants receive from the viticulturist. Most wine varieties produce higher quality grapes if grown under cool growing conditions in temperate latitudes or high altitudes. Warm to hot climates typically cause the grapes to be high in sugar and low in total acid, thus producing wines of 10-14% alcohol but flat in taste. One must, therefore, not always buy grapes by their varietal name. It is necessary to pay attention to the grapes' origin and always test them for acid and sugar content, even if it is by taste, before buying.

Yeast.

Wild yeast is found naturally on grapes. The 'bloom' or light white coating on grapes is a mixture of different wild yeast and bacteria. They are susceptible to SO2 (sulfide) and typically produce wines of 4-6% alcohol (unless natural conditions are altered). Natural fermentation can produce unique flavors or off tastes and spoilage due to the bacteria associated with them. Using a pure culture of domesticated yeast is preferable to make a cleaner, more uniform flavor.

Wine or domesticated yeast (*Saccharomyces cerevisiae*) are also found on grapes but in much fewer numbers. Wine yeast is facultative anaerobes (no alcohol is produced if one hundred percent is aerobic). They are more tolerant to alcohol and SO2 than the wild varieties. Many strains have been selected for different fermentation rates, but the flavor differences are slight. Other yeast species, such as *S. fermentii* or *S. bayanus*, are essential in flor sherry and other specialty wines.

Like all living things, yeast requires essential elements for growth:

1) Readily metabolized source of carbohydrate (i.e.

sucrose, glucose, fructose, but not starch),

2) Minerals-nitrogen source, phosphorus, and potassium,

3) Trace elements and

4) Vitamins.

Grape juice provides all the essentials yeast need to grow, divide, and convert sugar to alcohol. Many other fruit juices do not contain all these essential factors and are more difficult to ferment.

Unlike many other microorganisms, wine yeast thrives in acid solutions, like grape juice (pH 3.2-4.5). This was important in the past because no human pathogens could grow in wine, even if they were deliberately added. Therefore, mixing wine with polluted water was a way of producing safe drinking water.

Bacteria

Acetobacter aceti, or the acetic acid bacteria, are the bacteria that convert your homemade wine into homemade vinegar. *A. aceti* converts alcohol into acetic acid, which is called vinegar, in dilute amounts. Bacteria are ubiquitous and naturally occurring in grapes. They are obligate aerobes (i.e., they must have air to grow) and are very sensitive to SO_2. Bacteria are also inhibited by high alcohol (>14% by volume).

Lactobacillus or the lactic acid bacteria convert malic acid to lactic acid + CO_2. This fermentation is referred to as malo-lactic fermentation. Malo-lactic fermentation lowers the total acid content and raises the pH of the wine, which is desirable in high-acid wines and in the production of many fruit wines.

Lactobacillus is anaerobic (not needing air to survive).

III. FERMENTATION CHEMISTRY

The simple overall equation of fermentation was formulated in 1810 by Gay-Lussac as one molecule of sugar being converted into two molecules of ethanol and two molecules of CO_2 or

1 glucose $(C_6H_{12}O_2)$——>2 ethanol $(CH_3CH_2OH) + 2\ CO_2$

approximately 56 kilocalories of energy (given off as heat). Why should all this chemical mumbo jumbo be of any interest to the home winemaker? If one pays attention to the last two facts in the equation, we discover the necessity of learning this formula.

Fermentation releases large amounts of CO_2 gas. In large wineries, this has proven fatal more than once when people too close to a vigorously fermenting vat of wine were asphyxiated (suffocated). The CO_2 is given off so high that it looks like the wine is boiling. This is important to the home winemaker. He must choose a fermenting vessel at least 25% larger than the amount of wine one wants to ferment, to prevent the fermenting must from spilling out of the vessel. The chance of affixation at home is about zero.

The second important factor is the heat that is released. If a fermentation reaches 37°C, the heat will kill the yeast, causing a `stuck' fermentation. The addition of new yeast will restart the fermentation. Therefore, it is essential for good wine management to include a means to control the temperature of the fermentation.

IV. WINE AS ALCOHOL

It is of utmost importance to treat wine with respect and moderation. Of all the known alcohols in the world, only ethanol is the least poisonous to human beings. All the other alcohols cause grievous bodily damage, some even in minute amounts. Excess wine is toxic to our bodies.

Wine, however, is consumed wisely in moderation; it can be both enjoyable and healthful. The following are facts about the physiology of alcohol in the human system.

1) Alcohol acts as a depressant on the central nervous system. It is a "stimulant" only by removing our inhibitions.

2) The absorption is rapid and complete. It is absorbed more rapidly with the addition of carbon dioxide. This is the reason that sparkling wines make you drunk faster. Its effect on the body is controlled by the amount of food in your digestive system and your body weight.

.

3) Wine alcohol is rapidly absorbed into all body fluids, and its excretion (via urine) is minimal.

4) The liver metabolizes alcohol in our system. The maximum amount the liver can metabolize in a 24-hour period is 200 to 300 ml. High wine consumption leads to loss of appetite (and all the problems associated with it) and serious liver disease (Cirrhosis of the liver, which is fibrous scarring of the internal structure of the liver).

If it seems I have dwelt overlong on overindulgence on wine abuse (alcoholism), it is because of the seriousness of the problem, which is increasing throughout the world. It is not just a personal problem but a major social problem in many parts of the world. Worldwide, each year, thousands of people are killed by drunk drivers. Let us all take advice from our teacher and sage King Solomon from his Proverbs Chapter 23:20. "Be not among Winebibbers; among gluttonous coffers of meat; for the drunkard and the glutton shall come to poverty: and drowsiness shall clothe a man with rage."

V. GRAPES

The first thing the home winemaker must know about grapes is that only good grapes can make good wine. It is impossible to make a superior wine from inferior grapes, both technically and aesthetically. There are two types of grapes grown: table grapes, those used for fruit and making raisins) and wine grapes, which are used for making wine and brandy.

Figure 1, Anatomy of a grapevine

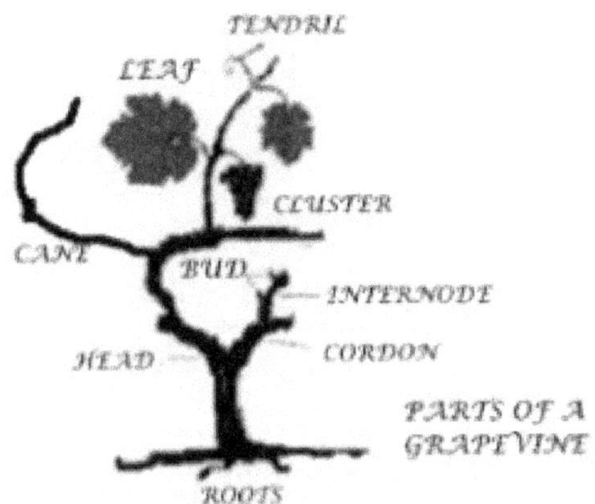

Table grapes (grapes for the fresh market) are large, high in soluble solids (fleshy), low in juice and total acid. They are picked at 14-16° Brix. Degrees Brix is the standard measurement of the total soluble solids in a fluid. In grapes, the sugar content of the juice makes up the vast majority of total soluble solids. They have a low ratio of skin surface to juice content.

Wine grapes are small in size, low in soluble solids, juicy, and high in total acidity. They have a high skin surface-to-juice ratio, which is essential for color extraction in red wines. Wine grapes are picked at 20-25° Brix.

Most wine grape varieties have white juice, whether they are white or red varieties. The red pigment in the grape skins gives the wine its red color. There are unique varieties with red juice. They are called teinturiers, such as Alicante

Bouchet, Royalty, and Rubired. It is possible to produce a light rose wine from a red variety by fermenting the juice without the skins.

Figure 2: Grape Cluster Anatomy

Below, I summarize the essential viticultural characteristics for home winemakers.

Viticultural Characteristics Important to Winemaking

23

Wine Type	Harvest Period	Taste & Aroma	Productivity
White Wine Varieties			
Chenin Blanc	Early – Mid*	N**	Med - High
French Colombard	Early	S - D	High
Sauvignon Blanc	Mid	D	Medium
Semillon	Mid	M	Medium
Emerald Riesling	Early - Mid	D	High
Muscat Canelli	Early	D	Low
Red Wine Varieties			

Royalty	Mid	S	High
Rubired	Mid	S	High
Cabernet Sauvignon	Late	D	Low
Carignan	Late	S	Large
Grenache	Mid	S	Large
Petite Sarah	Mid	D	Large
Pinot Noir	Early	D	Low

* Mid =middle season.

D = distinctive, M= moderate, S= slightly distinctive and N= neutral.

Why Varietal Wine Grapes?

Technically, the concept of a good wine is easy to define. However, individual tastes are subjective and impossible to describe. It is possible, however, to know that one varietal wine (wine made predominately from one particular variety) is better than another.

Each wine grape variety has its unique taste (or lack of it) and aroma, as seen in the table above. In a blind test, an experienced wine taster has the ability to identify a particular wine is based on those distinct flavors and aromas. This unique flavor and aroma may be reduced by factors like:

1) Poor quality grapes,

2) Diluting

a) Making the wine from 2 or more varieties or

b) Blending in more than 30% of another wine and

3) The addition of sugar, which will obscure the varietal flavor.

Sugar has a physiological effect on our taste buds. When sugar is present with other tastes, our taste buds absorb the sugar taste more than any other flavor, thus masking any unique varietal flavor that might have been present. This is one reason experienced wine drinkers prefer dry wines, i.e., to experience the distinctive taste of the wine. There is just one type of table wine in which it is desirable to leave residual sugar, i.e., Muscat. When Muscat is fermented to complete dryness it has a harsh, unpleasant bitter taste.

The quality of a unique varietal taste depends on the quality of the grapes and the winemaker. If the winemaker wants to produce a wine with a pronounced varietal flavor, he must use at least 30% of his grapes from the particular variety he plans to make the wine from. I recommend that the home winemaker use at least 90% of the varietal grape he or she chooses. Most blending is done for economic reasons. A bottle of wine labeled as being of a particular variety receives 50-200% more money than a generically labeled bottle. This makes using the legal minimum (51%) economically worthwhile in the short run.

How the Home Winemaker Selects Good Wine Grapes

1) Sugar Content. Any good viticulturist will have a refractometer for determining sugar content. Select grapes randomly from individual clusters and vines (or containers already picked). Pick 4~8 berries at random from 10-15 different clusters. Crush all the berries together and place a sample on the refractometer, which gives its readings in Brix. For wine between 11-13% alcohol, you want grapes between 20-23° Brix.

2) Acid Content.

The best criterion for selecting grapes is their Sugar-acid ratio. There are simple kits that can be used at home to provide you with the total acid content of your juice. The next best thing is an organoleptic test (acting on or involving using sense organs. Place a small sample of the juice in your mouth. Don't swallow it! The excess sugar will lower your ability to test further samples. Swish the sample around your mouth and then spit it out. Then rinse your mouth with water. The aim is to get a rough estimation of the total acidity. If the taste is flat, then the resultant wine will be flat. Kosher tartaric acid is available in Israel and the United States.

The adjustment of wine pH often involves the use of tartaric acid crystals. Winemakers typically employ a ratio of about 1 gram of these crystals per liter of wine to achieve a 0.1 reduction in pH. This translates to roughly 0.13 ounces per gallon. To illustrate, consider a scenario where you're working with a 19-liter batch of wine (equivalent to 5 gallons). To lower the pH from 3.6 to 3.4, you'd need to introduce approximately 38 grams of tartaric acid crystals to the mixture. For those more comfortable with imperial measurements, this amount is close to 1.3 ounces. This method allows precise control over the wine's acidity, which is crucial for achieving the desired flavor profile and ensuring proper preservation.

Adding it to your fermenting must is a possible way to increase your acid content. Another home solution is adding 10-15% less ripe or greenish grapes to your crushed grapes (which will be higher in acid).

3) Physical Quality of the grapes.

Closely examine the grapes for debris, contamination, and insect damage. All these can cause off tastes and odors in your wine.

4) Time of Harvest.

Pick your grapes at the coolest time of the day. The temperature of the grape juice influences the rate of fermentation. Grapes picked during the hottest period of the day will have a higher temperature and require more energy to cool them down to enable a controlled fermentation.

Seasonal Strategy:

Pay special attention to their ripening dates if you plan to make several wines in one season. There are two essential reasons. First, most home winemakers lack space to ferment more than one wine at a time. Therefore, select varieties allow you time to finish each operation with slight overlapping. Try to maintain at least three weeks between each new batch. The second reason is that grapes picked too late in their season will be high in sugar and low in acidity. This will produce a high-alcohol wine that has a flat taste.

Picking Grapes Yourself

Always pick grapes very early in the morning: 5-7:30 a.m. This ensures that the grapes will be cool and will help in the initial control of the fermentation temperature. If you are picking the grapes yourself, as mentioned above, try to include 8-15% unripe clusters. These should be fermented separately and used later for blending. Kosher tartaric acid is available to adjust the total acid content or pH.

Figure3.Hand harvesting grapes.

VI. KASHRUT AND WINE

Figure 4. Kiddush over wine

When concerned with wine, Kashrut means proper, suitable for use, fit for use, or permitted as food. Jewish law (Halacha) involves the planting of grapes and bottling of wine. Maintaining the kashrut of your wine requires that God-fearing Jews, such as Shomer Shabbat and Kashrut (religious Jews), handle the juice-wine from the moment you crush the grapes until you double seal the wine or boil it.

Five main areas of Halacha are important to winemaking, and they are:

1) *Orlah,*

2) *Ma'aser and T'rumot,*

3) *Avodah Zorah and*

4) *Kilahyim.*

5) Kosher Wine and Non-Jews: *Yai'in Mevushal*

Orlah:

Lev. 19:23 states: "Three years shall it be forbidden unto you. It shall not be eaten. 'When a new orchard or vineyard is planted, it is prohibited to use or gain any benefit from the fruit of the first three years. In the fourth year, the fruit was brought to the Temple as a sacrifice. The forbidden use of fruit from trees in the land of Israel and outside Israel is from the Torah, as Moshe Rabenu gave the Torah at Mt. Sinai.

If there is a doubt about whether the vineyard is orlah, it is forbidden in the land of Israel. However, outside of the land of Israel, if there is doubt about the age of the vineyard, then the fruit is permitted to be used. Today, because there is no Temple, our scholars have given us the right to use the fourth year's fruit. Any wine made from fruit from vines less than four years old will not be kosher,

Fruit trees produced by planting a seed, seeding, or moving a mature tree to another place are all required to observe three years of orlah.

Calculating the Age of a Fruit Tree

The Concept of Orla

Orla refers to the biblical prohibition against eating fruit from trees during their first three years of growth. This law is based on Leviticus 19:23-25.

Calculating Tree Age

1. **Initial Planting Date**
   - Trees planted at least 45 days before *Rosh Hashana* (by *Tu B'Av*) are considered one year old on that *Rosh Hashana*.
   - This gives the tree a "head start" in age calculation.
2. **Year Counting**
   - 1st Year: From planting (if before *Tu B'Av*) until the first *Rosh Hashana*.
   - 2nd Year: From first *Rosh Hashana* to second *Rosh Hashana*.
   - 3rd Year: From second *Rosh Hashana* to third *Rosh Hashana*

- ◦ 4th Year: Begins on the third *Rosh Hashana*

When Orla Ends:

- Fruit is permissible to eat if the tree's buds appear after *Tu B'Shvat* of the fourth year.
- This can result in a span as short as 2.5 years from planting to permissible fruit.

Example Timeline

Let's use a tree planted on *Tu B'Av*:

1. **1st Year:** (*Tu B'Av*) to (Rosh Hashana)
2. **2nd Year:** From Rosh Hashana until the next Rosh Hashana.
3. **3rd Year:** From Rosh Hashana until the next Rosh Hashana)
4. **4th Year:** Begins from Rosh Hashana.
   - ◦ Fruit from buds appearing after *Tu B'Shvat* are permissible

Key Points

- The 45-day rule before Rosh Hashana accelerates the age count.
- *Tu B'Shvat* in the fourth-year marks when new buds are considered post-Orla.
- This system allows fruit to be permissible in as little as 2.5 years after planting.

Ma'aser and Terumot:

Every food from which one must separate *Ma'aser and Terumot* is called tevel. This portion of the separated produce is forbidden to be eaten, according to Lev. 22:15, "and they shall not profane the holy things of the children of Israel which they offer to the Lord."

The procedure is as follows. 1) The people of Israel were obligated to give 10% of their produce to the Levites. Of this, the Levites were required to give 10% or 1% or the original to the Priests (*Cohanim*). The people of Israel were also required to give 1% to the Cohanim. Since the destruction of the Holy Temple, our sages have allowed us to redeem what would have been given to the Levites with a coin instead. This coin is then disposed of in a proper manner so that no one can benefit from it. At present, we are required to give the 2% that would have been given to the Cohanim.

The actual blessing and methods are listed below.

Fruits requiring the removal of Offering and Tithes.

In general, it is forbidden to eat or use all fruit or vegetables grown in the land of Israel without offerings and tithes. However, some rules define more precisely what fruit must be tithed and some fruit exemptions (E. Melamed).

Separating the fruit one says. Blessed are You, Lord our God, King of the universe, who has sanctified us with His commandments and has commanded us to separate offerings and tithes.

ולפני שימר את נוסח הפדיון מעשר שני, אם מעשר טבל ודי יברך גם ברכה זו:

ברוך אתה י-י אלוקנו מלך העולם, אשר קדשנו בצותיו וציונו

על פדיון מעשר שני.

נוסח הפרשת תרומות ומעשרות: לוקח הפירות מעט יותר מאחוז ומבדילו מן הפירות ואומר:

יותר מאחד שיש כאן הרי הוא תרומה גדולה בצד צפונו (אם מעשר כמה מינים יחד יאמר- כל מין על מינו): אותו אחד ממאה שיש כאן ועוד תשעה חלקים כמותו בצד צפונו של הפירות (אם מעשר כמה מינים יחד יאמר- כל מין על מינו): אותו אחד ממאה שיש כאן תשעה חלקים כמותו בצד אותו אחד ממאה שיש כאן ועוד תשעה חלקים כמותו בצד צפונו של הפירות (אם מעשר כמה מינים יחד יאמר- כל מין על מינו) הרי הוא מעשר ראשון:

אותו אחד ממאה שעשיתו מעשר ראשון, עשוי תרומה מעשר (אם מעשר כמה מינים יחד יאמר – כל מין על מינו)" ומעשר עני בצד דרומו (אם מעשר כמה מינים יחד יאמר- כל מין על מינו), ואם צריך מעשר שני יהא מעשר שני בדרומו (אם מעשר כמה מינים יחד יאמר- כל מין על מינו), ומחלל הוא וחומשו על פריטה בט=מטבע שיחדתיה לחילול מעשר שני:

אם הוא רבעי יהא מחלל הוא וחומשו על פרוט במטבע שיחדתיה לחילל מעשר.

An important distinction should be made. When the intention is to use the fruit, then *Ma'asrot and Terumot* are taken from the entire lot. However, if a fruit product, such as juice, wine, or brandy, is the goal, then the Ma'asort and Terumot are taken from the final product. It is necessary to remove Ma'asort and Terumot at the end of the wine-making process before bottling them when they are fit to drink.

Avodah Zorah:

It is forbidden to practice *Avodah Zorah* or idol worship in any form, even if your life is endangered. It is one of the three prohibitions that cannot be mitigated by danger to your life. To avoid *Avodah Zorah*, our sages discouraged intimate contact between Jews and non-Jews. It was and still is common practice among the Gentiles to bless and use wine as offerings (libations) to their idols and icons. Wine blessed by goyim or used in libations is known as *yien nesach*. Even today, in the Catholic Church, the wine represents the blood of J—-s; Wine fit for use by Jews has to be meticulously kept separate from any gentile to prevent the adulteration of the wine and, through its use, lead one to idol worship. Therefore, there are strict rules involved in winemaking, from when the grapes are crushed until the wine is bottled. Even wine made by goyim for non-religious purposes has the same prohibitions as *yien nesach*.

Rabbi Moses ben Maimon (RAMBAM) codified most winemaking laws. Any wine touched by a heathen, i.e., idol-worshipper, is forbidden to be used in any form. The Rambam did not include Moslems in this category. Wine touched by heathens is prohibited for consumption, and no benefit may be derived from it. What makes up the act of a heathen touching the wine, rendering it prohibited? He must touch the wine with his hand or any other organ in which it is customary to pour out heathen libations and shake it. However, if a heathen touches the wine on purpose to cause damage to a Jew, then it is the same as anything that has been damaged on purpose. Wine is still forbidden but can be sold to heathens for your benefit.

The ramifications and exact situations are numerous and complex and do not fall within the scope of this book, but a few things are necessary to mention. From when the grapes are crushed until the wine is boiled or bottled with a double seal, the wine and its vessels should not be touched by non-Jews. Direct Contact with the wine should be carried out by religious Jews who understand all the laws involved in winemaking so as not to make the wine unfit for consumption unintentionally.

A Jew may deposit his wine with a heathen in a closed vessel, but on the condition that it has two identification marks, known as a seal within a seal. In modern wine practice, this is observed by Jews and non-Jews alike. The first seal is the cork or screw cap, and the second seal is the plastic cover over the mouth and cork of the bottle. Once the vessel is double-sealed, anyone can handle the wine, and it is still permissible to consume it and to derive benefit from it.

Kilahyim:

The term Kilahyim means a mixture of two kinds. The laws of *Kilahyim* deal with forbidden mixtures such as:

1) The sowing and grafting of heterogeneous plants in

the same field, orchard, or vineyard,

2) The hybridization of different animals and the

working of mixtures of animals together and

3) The forbidden use of wool and flax (linen) in a

garment that will be used for clothing.

Grafting of two diverse species is forbidden, but the fruit may be eaten if it exists. The prohibition of *Kilahyim* as applies to vineyards growing in the land of Israel is from the Torah, and outside Israel is from our scholars (חז"ל).

In our case, the prohibition of growing diverse species next to each other is different. It depends on the arrangement of the vines. The question is whether it is a few scattered vines or whether a vineyard is a concern. The schools of Hillel and Shamai discussed the problem of what constitutes a vineyard in *Mishne Kilahyim* in chapter section 6. The school of Hillel concludes that the minimum number of vines to make a vineyard is 5. To call five wines a vineyard, the grapes need to be planted in the following pattern:

      *   *

   *

     *   *

Four *amahs (1 amah = 58 cm, and six tefachim = 1 amah) or 2.12 meters must be allowed before the* seed can be sown between the rows. Where the situation does not form a vineyard, a mere six *tefachim* is necessary between the vine and another cultivated plant.

A vineyard in which *Kilahyim* is found causes part of the vineyard to become forfeit. All vines within 16 *amot (i.e.,* 9.28 meters) diameter need to be destroyed.

It is forbidden to use or derive any benefit from grapes that grow in a vineyard where *Kilahyim* is found. Wine made from a vineyard in which Kilahyim exists is strictly forbidden and not kosher.

Figure 5. An example of *Kilahyim*: Cherry trees growing in a vineyard in California

Kosher Wine and Non-Jews.

Even today, the Catholic Church uses wine in its ceremonies. In ancient times, wine was an essential part of sacrifices for both Jews and non-Jews. Since non-Jews used wine for sacrificial purposes connected with the very stringent laws against idol worship, the Sages decreed that any open bottle of wine touched by a non-Jew was no longer kosher. This was due to doubting that the non-Jew had made a blessing over the wine to his gods.

However, one exception is *Yayin Mevushal* (Boiled Wine). Kosher wine (or grape juice) that has been boiled before the bottling process is called *yayin mevushal*. During the time of the *Beit Hamikdash* (the Holy Temple in Jerusalem), cooking wine rendered it unfit to be brought to the Altar.

Therefore, Yayin Mevushal is not considered a "sacramental wine." This excludes it from the prohibition against handling by non-Jews. These wines must bear the symbol of a reliable supervision organization, and it should be printed on the bottle that it is Yayin Mevushal.

VII. HOME WINEMAKING OPERATIONS

43

Summary of Operations

The operations involved in home winemaking are exactly parallel to those of commercial operations except on a much smaller scale. Below is a list of all the steps involved in making home wine.

Analysis of the grapes, sugar-acid ratio, and

damage to the grapes (from birds, insects or

disease).

Preparing the Grapes for Fermentation:

harvest, crush, and destem.

Sulfuring.

Fluid Recovery and pressing.

Fermentation-natural vs. induced.

Sugar-alcohol conversion

Transfer and racking.

Special operations—addition of spirits or

sugar and pH adjustment.

Tartrate Stabilization—removal of excess

Potassium bitartrate crystals.

Aging—glass, wood, stainless steel.

Clarification, sedimentation, and fining.

Blending.

Bottling

Each phase of the wine-making process and the necessary equipment will be explained below.

The first step, choosing grapes, will be skipped since it has already been discussed in the previous section. Remember to have small hand pruning shears to remove any diseased or damaged grapes from the clusters. Insects can hide between and on the grapes inside the cluster. Wash the grapes and allow the excess water to drain off before crushing.

Figure 6. Mealy bug infected cluster

2. Preparing the Grapes for Fermentation

Once you have harvested the grapes, the next step is to crush and prepare them for fermentation. Knowing when the grapes were last sprayed and with what pesticide is essential. Washing the grapes before use may be necessary if recently sprayed with a long-lasting pesticide. Your crush should be done in a place close to where your fermentation will be carried out. There should be sufficient room and water accessible for cleaning up afterward. The easiest and most ancient method of crushing grapes (in small amounts) is with your feet. Wash your feet well before crushing. One can crush by hand, but it is not feasible for more than 8 kgs of grapes. It is physically challenging and tiring work. There are small electrical and hand-driven Crushers available to the home winemaker. These items are available in any shop that sells equipment for winemaking.

Figure 7. Home grape-crushing equipment

The vessel you crush your grapes should be at least 10 cm deep. It shouldn't be too large to make transferring to your fermenting vat challenging. Use any stainless steel, wood (waterproof), or food-grade plastic containers. Avoid copper, zinc, tin, and bronze vessels, as they give off heavy metals that can be poisonous to the consumer or detrimental to the wine. The next significant operation is to destroy the crushed grapes and remove all the stems and leaves from the crushed grapes. This is done immediately after each batch of grapes is crushed. Run your hands through the crushed mixture, catching the stems between your fingers. Have a garbage can handy for immediate disposal. Stems covered in grape juice readily attract flies and other insects. Stems and leaves give a grassy taste to the wine and add excessive tannins. Tannins are one factor that gives a harsh flavor to the wine.

3. Sulfuring

Sulfur, as sulfur dioxide (SO_2), can be used in two different stages of the wine-making process. First, it can be added immediately after crushing to kill all the naturally occurring microorganisms (yeast and bacteria) and act as an antioxidant, and/or it can be added at the end of the fermentation for the same reasons.

Air, i.e., oxygen, is wine's no. 1 enemy. Exposure to air causes a chemical reaction known as oxidation. This oxidation may be induced by enzymes in the fruit or by a direct reaction between phenolic compounds in the must and oxygen from the air. Sulfur dioxide reduces the oxidation-reduction potential of the juice or wine. Sulfur dioxide is a strong enough reducing agent that is oxidized in preference to the phenolic compounds in the must. Only free sulfur dioxide is reactive. Therefore, the ratio between bound and free sulfur dioxide is essential. The amount of free sulfur dioxide depends on temperature, amount of sugar, aldehyde, and the pH of the juice or wine. This oxidation causes a burnt-like taste and turns the wine a brown color. This is particularly bad for white wines, but in some red wines, it is encouraged (port). Sulfur can be added in many forms, but the most available to the home winemaker is potassium meta-bisulfate. It is available as a powder and can be added directly into the grape juice or make sure the SO_2 is thoroughly mixed into the must. The amount of free (active) SO_2 available from potassium meta-bisulfate is 50%. Therefore, if 100 ppm (ppm=parts per million) of SO_2 is required, you need to add 200 ppm of K-meta-bisulfate. The usual range of SO_2 in wine is 75-150 ppm, whereas the upper range is used for particularly spoiled grapes or wine that may suffer excessive exposure to air. Be exceedingly careful with the addition of SO_2 because an excess causes the wine to have a burnt match smell.

If you want natural fermentation, do not add SO_2 because it will kill all the natural yeast. However, if you plan to inoculate with a pure culture of domesticated yeast, it is essential to kill off the entire wild microflora so they won't compete with the domesticated yeast. One should wait two to three hours after adding SO_2 before adding the domesticated yeast culture. The amount of potassium meta-bisulfate needed for 10 liters of must is shown in the table below.

Amounts of Sulfur Dioxide to Add to Musts

Maturity of Grapes	Condition	ppm	Equivalent in teaspoons
Under ripe	Clean	75	1/3
Mature	Clean	100	1/2
Overripe	Moldy	125	3/5

If you have a scale available, it is preferable to use exact measurements to avoid excessive amounts.

After fermentation has finished, the addition of sulfur dioxide is recommended for all wines. It is crucial not to add too much SO_2 since it causes an unpleasant odor. Adding between 75-125 ppm is recommended, depending on the condition of the wine. SO_2 gives lasting protection against enzymatic oxidation but little against non-enzymatic oxidation (due to slow exposure to air (and, therefore, does not interfere with the aging process.

Sorbic acid is used both instead of and in conjunction with sulfur dioxide. It is very effective in preventing malo-lactic fermentation in wine while in storage. Sorbic acid excess will also produce unpleasant odors. Control of yeast growth in sweet table wines can be obtained by using 80 ppm of sorbic acid and 30 ppm of SO_2 together. Sorbic acid's sensory threshold is around 135 ppm, but some people are sensitive to it as low as 50 ppm. Therefore, the recommended dosage of sorbic acid and sulfur dioxide together should not exceed 125 ppm. Sorbic acid itself should not exceed 90 ppm and should not be less than 70 ppm.

Fumaric acid is also used to prevent malo-lactic fermentation. Fumaric acid at the rate of 1.5gm/Liter with 75 ppm SO_2 has been found to be very effective as an antiseptic. Using fumaric acid also increases the total titratable acid.

4 Fluid Recovery:

Here, it will be necessary to define several terms to understand the following processes.

a) The term must refer to both the solution of crushed grapes to be fermented and the fermenting solution itself. The term wine is used for the liquid upon completion of fermentation.

In white wines, must is the grapes' juice after pressing, and in red wines, must is a mixture of juice, skins, and seeds.

b) Pomace is the solid waste material remaining after pressing. The pressing causes it to form cakes. It contains all the skins, stems, seeds, and debris.

c) Free Run is the must that exists from the crush without pressing. It is often fermented separately in high-quality wineries. Pressing releases many more materials (such as tannins, which add harshness) that would not be found in the free run.

A ton of grapes yields 550-700 liters of juice with an average of around 640 liters. Dry pomace averages about 5% of the total weight. The efficiency of the total yield of must depends upon the variety in question and on how the must is pressed from the skins. Place 2-3 kg of must in 2-4 layers of gauze and squeeze out the must for small amounts of wine. It is advisable to use a press for large quantities of wine (over 100 liters). It is essential to have a means of waste disposal available, because like the stems, pomace quickly attracts insects.

Figure 8. Fluid recovery of must from crushed grapes.

5. Fermentation:

Fermentation is the conversion of sugar to alcohol (ethanol) by yeast. In the process (as mentioned above), CO_2 and heat are given off. The control of this heat is essential in winemaking. Temperature is the prime control of the rate of fermentation. White wines need low temperatures (8-14°C) to retain good aroma and flavors. White wines ferment much longer than red wines. Depending on the variety, red wines can be fermented at 20-30°C. Once the temperature reaches 37°C, it kills the yeast, and the fermentation stops. This is known as a 'stuck' fermentation and can be restarted by allowing the must to cool and the addition of a pure yeast starter. During fermentation, the temperature rises 1-1.25°C for every drop of 1° Brix.

For example, we can start with grapes of 24° Brix at a temperature of 25°C. The fermentation of 24° Brix must will produce 24-32° of heat. Without a means of controlling the fermentation, you will reach 37°C and a stuck fermentation.

How to control fermentation temperature? For white wines, which are fermented without skins, the fermentation temperature can be controlled by various types of refrigeration of the vessel or the entire fermentation area. This is generally difficult for the home winemaker to do and is one reason I recommend only those people with proper equipment to make white wines at home. Small amounts of white wine can be fermented in your home refrigerator. Ferment during the day inside the refrigerator, and in the evening, when the temperature has fallen to 14°C, allow the must to ferment outside till the morning. This is not ideal, but passable. If an old refrigerator can be adjusted to 8-14° C, it would be the best situation, but still, only a maximum of 40 liters can be produced.

Red wines are much easier for the home winemaker to handle. Initial fermentation may take place in the open. One should use containers that allow the generated heat to escape. Red wines are initially fermented with the skins to extract the color. The skins, seeds, and stems create the components of the cap. This cap acts as an efficient insulator, which captures most of the heat and some of the CO_2. Managing the cap is, therefore, the key to temperature control of red wines. The cap should be broken up and mixed back into the fermenting must at least 2, preferably 3 times a day, morning and evening.

Figure 9. Fermentation of red grapes in a plastic container with a thermometer.

This breaks up the insulating action, allowing the heat to escape. Breaking the cap provides better skin contact for the extraction of color. This is done by punching down the cap and mixing it back into the must, stirring it with a stick about 30% longer than the vessel's depth. In commercial wineries, this is done by pumping the must from beneath the cap and spraying the wine over the cap.

6. Sugar-alcohol conversion:

Table wines fermented to complete dryness will produce alcohol at a rate of 0.55 % alcohol for every degree Brix. Example: must, which starts at 24° Brix, will create a wine of 13.2% alcohol. With this conversion rate, you can pick (or buy) your grapes to make the exact amount of alcohol you desire.

Fermentation should always be carried out on a platform to ensure ease of transferring the wine (by gravitation) in later operations. Fermentation can be accomplished in any food-grade container large enough to be not more than 1/2- 3/4 full. This prevents must from spilling out when it is actively fermenting.

There are three basic types of fermentation they are:

A) Natural

b) Controlled

C) Maceration Carbonique.

a) Natural Fermentation.

The 'bloom' or the light whitish powder found on all grapes is a mixture of wild yeast and bacteria. This indigenous yeast can ferment grape must. The procedure is simple: crush the grapes, allow the natural yeast population to increase, and conduct fermentation. Natural fermentation takes a few days longer to conduct since active fermentation does not occur until the yeast population has increased to a sufficient number. This is the oldest and simplest method of making wine and, technically, for quality control, the poorest. First, since no SO_2 is added, there is no protection against bacterial fermentation, which can produce off-tastes, foul odors, and potentially dangerous chemicals. Second, oxidation is a greater risk in natural fermentation because of the time-lapse till active fermentation. The oxidation problem can be partly overcome by adding 5-10 active starters from an ongoing natural fermentation, but there will be oxidation damage to the starter.

Third, wild yeast rarely ferments to above 5% alcohol. This leaves the wines open to secondary fermentations, mostly malo-lactic, which will lower the acid content of the wine, and the lack of acid is already a general problem in Israeli wines. The fourth problem is taste and aroma. With wild yeast, there is no control over the unique flavors and aromas that might develop. They may range from uniquely unusual and pleasant to bad-smelling and undrinkable. Natural fermentation is the easiest but least dependable method.

B. Controlled Fermentation.

By definition, controlled fermentation is a fermentation regulated and manipulated by man, in our case to produce a uniform reproducible product called wine.

Step 1. Remove all diseased and spoiled grapes.

Step 2. Crush and destem the grapes.

Step 3. Add 75-120 ppm SO_2 in whatever form you prefer. For white wines whose grapes are in good condition, no more than 100 ppm SO_2 is needed. For red wine, add 75-100 ppm SO_2. Only use high dosages of SO_2 if there are a lot of contaminated grapes. Remember, however, excessive SO_2 causes the 'burnt match' smell.

Step 4. Wait 1-1.5 hours before adding pure yeast starter. A yeast starter is made by adding a culture of pure wine yeast to a liter of freshly squeezed grape juice. Once it ferments, it's used to inoculate ten liters of grape juice until you have between 3-5% of the total amount of wine you will be making. Making the starter from the same variety you will ferment or some neutral variety like Sultanina is preferable. This should all be started 2-3 weeks before your planned fermentation. Initial active fermentation can take place in an open vessel.

Step 5. After 8-12 days (for refrigerated fermentations, it will be longer), transfer the fermenting must into a closed container with an airlock.

Step 6. When fermentation has finished (no more bubbles are evident in the airlock), add more SO_2 at a rate of 70-100 ppm. The amount added depends on how well one can minimize air contact. If you have proper equipment and work fast, then don't add more than 85 ppm SO_2; if not, use around l00 ppm.

C. Maceration Carbonique

Step 1 In maceration carbonique (recommended only for red wines), the whole berries are placed/al in a closed container, the fermenting vessel, and brought under anaerobic conditions, i.e., fermentation takes place in the absence of air. This is achieved by sealing the fermenting vessel hermetically. Under these conditions, the fruit's metabolism changes from aerobic to anaerobic, and fermentation starts inside the skin. This should be allowed to continue for 8-10 days until the must have reached 4-5% alcohol.

Step 2 Prepare 3-5% pure yeast starter to be ready at the end of the ten days of anaerobic fermentation.

Step 3 After 8-10 days of anaerobic fermentation, crush, destem, and press the grapes.

Step 4 Add 75-120 ppm SO_2 and wait 2-3 hours.

Step 5 Add the actively fermenting pure wine yeast starter to the must. The rest of the procedures are identical to those in a controlled fermentation.

The process of maceration carbonique produces wines with the following characteristics:

a) Fresh fruity taste,

b) Low tannins,

c) A unique flavor as compared to a regular fermentation

and

d) Short-lived wines.

The flavor of these wines deteriorates after 18 months. This method of fermentation is recommended for wine that will not be aged and drunk within ten months of bottling.

7. Transfer and Racking

The next major operation after fermentation is transferring and separating the wine from all the solid particles suspended in it. This process is called racking. Its purpose is to remove dead yeast, seeds, pieces of stems, and assorted floating solid particles.

Step 1 After fermentation, the wine is allowed to settle by gravitation for 8-10 days.

Step 2 As the wine settles, a thick layer of mud-like material begins to collect at the bottom of the vessel. This material is known as lees. This comprises all the solid particles mentioned above. A food-grade plastic hose can now be inserted into the closed container, and the clear wine siphoned off, leaving behind the lees. This process may need to be repeated 2-4 times, allowing the wine to settle successively longer each time (up to 3-6 weeks).

Now, it is essential that the home winemaker have as many bottles or containers of different sizes available as possible. Each time you rack the wine, the total amount left is less; therefore, if left in the same containers, there will be damage due to oxidation (exposure to air). Always keep the vessels holding the wine full and sealed as tight as possible.

8. Special Operations.

At this stage of the wine-making process, one begins many chemical manipulations. Each operation will be discussed, and the methodology will be explained.

a) Addition sugar: Sugar can be added at this stage for

two reasons:

1) For sweetening wines that have fermented to dryness

and

2) For starting a secondary yeast fermentation (in the b

bottle or bulk) for producing sparkling wines.

This will be discussed in the section on sparkling wines.

The home winemaker needs to use wines with a high alcohol content of 13-15% to avoid unwanted secondary fermentation in the bottle. Low-alcohol wines with residual sugar can be preserved by sterile filtration, which is unavailable to most home winemakers. Using overripe grapes to make sweet wine does not always produce the desired effect. The sweetness of your wine is an individual matter of taste. Therefore, each winemaker must empirically adjust the sugar amount until the desired result is achieved.

Dissolve sugar in a small volume of wine and then add the mixture back into the bulk of the wine. Mix thoroughly and then sample the wine. Repeat this as many times as necessary. There is no way to reverse this procedure. It is, therefore, recommended that about 10% of the wine be kept aside until you are sure you have reached the desired level of sweetness. If you exceed the desired level, you will have 10%, which is the amount of sweetness you want to dilute back down.

You can also buy a residual sugar home test kit. This simple test kit will give you an accurate reading of the sugar content in your wine.

b) Dilution: Home winemakers who desire a lower-alcohol wine and don't mind losing some of the taste can add water to the wine to reduce the alcohol content. This is not legal for commercial enterprises. Use filtered, bacteria-free, or sterile boiled water to dilute the wine. This caution is necessary because, with the reduced alcohol content, the wine is more susceptible to unwanted secondary fermentations and contaminations.

C) Addition of Acid: In warm areas like California, Israel, Australia, and South Africa, most European varieties bred for northern climates produce high-acid wines. However, the wines can be flat without sufficient acid in colder regions, such as northern and central Europe and the northeastern United States. Technically sound wine should have a good acid balance according to the characteristics of the variety.

Low-acid wines, which are flat-tasting, can be caused by the lack of acid in the grapes or by secondary malo-lactic fermentation. Total acid content is easy to measure at home, and investing in a small amount of equipment and chemicals is worthwhile for the serious home winemaker.

However, if one doesn't want to invest in the equipment and/or kits, one must test organoleptically and adjust.

Today, there are simple wine acid test kits with simple instructions. The acid most used for altering the acidic component of your wine is tartaric

acid. Citric and malic acid can be used but are less successful. Make sure that your tartaric acid has a stamp that it is kosher. Tartaric acid is made exclusively from wine.

Below is a table that provides guidelines for the amount of acid needed to produce a well-balanced wine. The amounts are given in the percent of titratable acid as tartaric acid.

Recommended Acid Content for Different Wines

Wine Types	Acid Content
Red	0.6-0.9%
Rose'	0.7-0.9%
White	0.8-1..0%
Dessert	0.4-0.65%
Sparkling Wines	9.7-1.0%

If commercial kosher tartaric is unavailable, the home winemaker can make and use a natural substitute. As grapes ripen, their acid content drops. Harvest 10-15% of your total harvest at 16° Brix when the grapes still have a high acid content and ferment this separately. When you reach the stage mentioned above, determine how much high-acid wine you want to blend in by adding a small amount at a time. The advantage of this system is that you are adding a hundred percent natural source of acid along with its varietal flavors and aromas.

If you should, by accident, add too much acid, all is not lost. $CaCO_2$, calcium carbonate, is excellent for -removing tartaric acid from wine. It works so well, and you must use this product with great care to not remove too much acid. Add the calcium carbonate and mix the wine thoroughly. It will slowly settle to the bottom as calcium tartrate. Allow the wine to settle for 10-14 days, and then rack the clear wine off the accumulated on the bottom of the vessel.

For instance, if the titratable acidity of the wine (or juice) is 1.2% (parts per hundred), you can determine the amount of calcium carbonate required to neutralize the total acidity in one gallon. The calculation would be: 1.2 x 10 x 2.4 = 28.8 grams of calcium carbonate needed to neutralize all the acid in a gallon.

d) pH:

The pH is a scale of 1-12 for measuring the amount of acid or base in a solution. The lower end of the scale being 1 to 7 is progressively less acid (H+) until you hit neutral at pH 7. The upper end of the scale, 7 to 12, is being progressively more basic (OH-). pH is critical to home winemakers.

The reasons are:

A low pH (acid) adds bacterial resistance to the wine since bacteria cannot grow well at a pH of 4 or below.

2) The pH of the wine controls the amount of free sulfur dioxide. The lower the pH, the more free SO_2 there is available. Some authorities don't recommend the addition of SO_2 for musts with a pH below 3.1

3) The tint of the color is affected, especially in red wines and

4) pH plays a vital role in the acid taste and sourness of the wine.

The pH of most wines ranges between 3 and 3.8. Table wines should have a pH of less than 3.5, and dessert wines less than 3.8. Wines with a pH of less than 3.4 are more resistant to spoilage, taste fresher and fruitier, and have a better shade of color.

The test for pH is by far the simplest. There is a special paper

called Litmus paper, which changes color when placed into a solution. The color depends on the solution pH. It is available from almost all firms that supply biological equipment and chemicals. Clear directions are given in each package, and a scale is provided. I recommend two sets of test papers, one general, with a range of 1-7, and one specific, with a range of 3-4; the pH of a must can be adjusted downward (made acidic) with the addition of tartaric acid.

Example: To adjust the pH of a must from 3.6 to 3.4, about 43 grams of tartaric acid is needed per 10 liters of must or wine. To raise the pH of a low-pH wine or must, add calcium carbonate (see use of calcium carbonate above).

e) Addition of Alcohol: If one wants to produce dessert wines, this is the stage to add wine spirits to the wine. The alcohol content of dessert wines ranges from 15% to 13%. Exact details and calculations will be discussed in the section on dessert wines.

9. Tartrate Stabilization

Grape juice is high in tartaric acid and potassium. As the juice is converted into alcohol, the wine becomes a supersaturated solution of potassium tartrate (cream of tartar). Sand-like potassium bitartrate crystals form in the wine and gravitate to the bottom of the wine vessel. The result is unpleasant for anyone drinking the wine (no one likes sand in their wine).

While still in bulk containers, wine should be stabilized for excess K-bitartrate. The procedure is simple but challenging for the home winemaker. In commercial wineries, the temperature of the wine is reduced to -4 to -5 $^{\circ}$C and is held at that temperature for 10-14 days. At home, without special equipment, it is possible to stabilize the wine in the refrigerator in small lots of 5-10 liters. Keep the wine refrigerated until you see the excess k-bitartrate sediment at the bottom of the vessel. Then rack off the clear wine off the crystals. Another method can be used if the wine is not stored for more than 10-15 months. Rack the wine before bottling; if it is not subjected to frigid temperatures, it should hold for 10-15 months. These crystals can be purified (consult the Merck Index) and used the following season as tartaric acid.

10. Aging

The purpose of aging is to mellow the harsh tastes of red wines. Several varieties, when young, have a high content of tannins. Prolonged aging causes the tannins to oxidize and reduce the harshness.

One method of controlling slow oxidation is by aging the wine in wooden barrels. The aging of wine is conducted in oak barrels or corked bottles. In large commercial enterprises, large glass-lined containers are sometimes used. Aging in oak adds a vanilla-like taste to the wine. Generally, white and rose wines are not aged in wood. Not all red wines improve with wood aging. Among the leading wines commonly aged in wood are Ruby Cabernet, Cabernet Sauvignon, Merlot, Petite Sarah, Pinot Noir, and many more. All the other wines improve to a point with bottle aging. Today, aging varies from 3 to 18 months in wood and 3 to 36 months in the bottle. Today, a commercial bottle of wine over 4-5 years old is uncommon and expensive if available.

The length of aging depends on the desired effect of the individual winemaker. Aging should be done in a dry cool, preferably dark place. The wine should not be exposed to direct sunlight. If you are aging in the bottle, lay it on its side. This keeps the cork moist, which helps it to maintain its swollen size and, therefore, form an effective seal against oxidation. Bottles with screw caps for seals should not be stored for long periods. They are very susceptible to oxidation since the seal is ineffective against air.

Why age at all? It is believed that a very slow diffusion of oxygen is carried out through the wood, slow enough to avoid damage due to oxidation. This limited oxidation produces desirable changes and contributes to flavor and extracts, causing the wine to become more complex while mellowing many of the harsh flavors. Depending on the relative humidity, the water and alcohol content slowly evaporate, causing an air space to form in the barrels. This air space is known as "head space". Managing the headspace is an integral part of the aging process. Adding wine to fill up the barrel is known as "topping; constant topping off of the barrels is extremely important. The longer the wine is exposed to air, the greater the damage due to oxidation. Barrels must be regularly topped off every 2-4 weeks. It is necessary to have many different-sized vessels to keep them full since the amount of wine constantly changes. By law, one may use a different type of wine for topping off barrels. In some modern wineries where wine is stored in bulk, wine is maintained with a layer of inert gas such as nitrogen or carbon dioxide to prevent oxidation.

Wood aging of red wines is recommended for experienced winemakers. One must know how to prepare and maintain a barrel properly. Oak barrels take extra space, skill, and work. They also add significant expense to winemaking.

11. Clarification

Clarification is the process by which all the fine particles, called colloids, suspended in the wine are removed. These colloids induce turbidity (cloudiness) in the wine. The more precise the wine, the cleaner the taste, and the more aesthetic pleasure one can get from his or her efforts.

It is rare for a wine to become brilliantly clear by natural settling. Fining agents are added in small amounts, which absorb or combine chemically and physically with the colloids to neutralize their electric charges, causing them to agglomerate and gravitate to the bottom of the vessel with time. The home winemaker has a choice of several different fining agents from which to choose:

1) Bentonite, which is diatomaceous earth,

2) egg white

3) Kosher gelatin

4) Activated charcoal

5) Kosher casein and a

6) Number of commercially protein-based fining agents.

The common most used fining agent is Bentonite. It is effective at removing proteins or peptide materials. Activated charcoal, gelatin, casein, and others may be also used and assist in removing unstable tannins and other pigments.

The amount of fining agent added is between 0.01-0.015%w/v. Tests on small portions of wine should be made to determine the optimum dosage for each individual wine. The protein binds the colloids, forming a coaglum, which slowly settles to the bottom over several days to a few weeks. This leaves the wine clear with sediment of coagulum on the bottom of the vessel. This is removed by racking off the clear wine.

The amount of tannins in the wine is a major factor in this reaction. Insufficient tannin or an excess of clarifying agent can retard the clarification of the wine.

Red wines, which, by nature, are high in tannin, generally clarify well, and this process removes some of the astringency caused by the tannin may be desirable since it mimics, to some extent, the aging process. White wines may need tannin added to achieve an efficient, satisfactory clarification. Note that most clarifying agents reduce the intensity of the color of red wines and lighten the color of white wines.

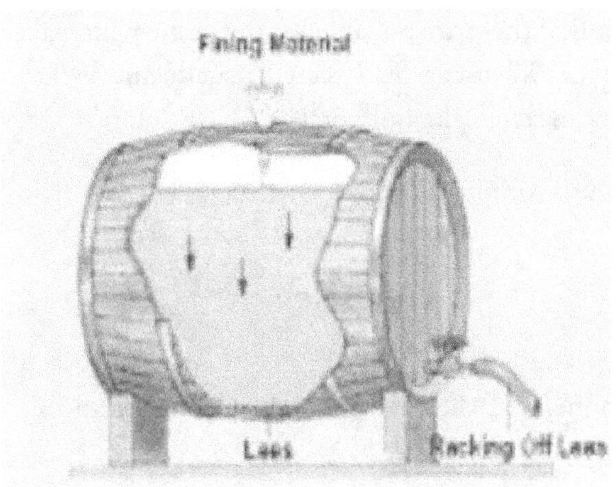

Figure 10. How Fining Agents Work

12. Blending

There is often variation in flavor, color, and alcohol content of various types of wine made in the same year. To produce a uniform product in which each bottle will be as good (we hope) as the previous one, it is desirable to blend the various lots. The amount of tannin, total acid, sugar, alcohol, and volatile acids partly controls the wine's flavor. Not all of these are possible for the home winemaker to analyze with limited resources. What can be detected visually and by taste without difficulty is the amount of sugar, alcohol, total acid, and color.

There is a simple algebraic formula for blending:

A = m-b

B = a-m

A = the weight of one component of the mixture and its concentration in percent = `a`,

B = the Weight of the second component of the mixture and its concentration in percent = `b`.

m = the desired percent of the factor to be blended.

Example:

Suppose one has two lots of wine. The first lot has 14% alcohol, and the second lot has 11% alcohol. You desire a wine with 13% alcohol.

In this situation a = 14, b = 11, m = 13. Then A = m-b = 13-11=2 B = a-m = 14-13=1

or one needs twice the amount of lot A than of lot B to reach the desired alcohol level of 13%.

Pearson Square Method:

Another easy method is a geometric representation that can be used to compute the ratio of two mixture ingredients.

Step 1. First, draw a simple rectangle:

Step 2. In the upper left-hand corner, place the concentration of one ingredient. In the lower left-hand corner, put the concentration of the second ingredient. In the center, write the desired concentration and subtract diagonally from the direction of the right side.

Example: One lot of wine contains 11.5% alcohol, the second 14% alcohol. The desired concentration is 12.5% alcohol.

Solution

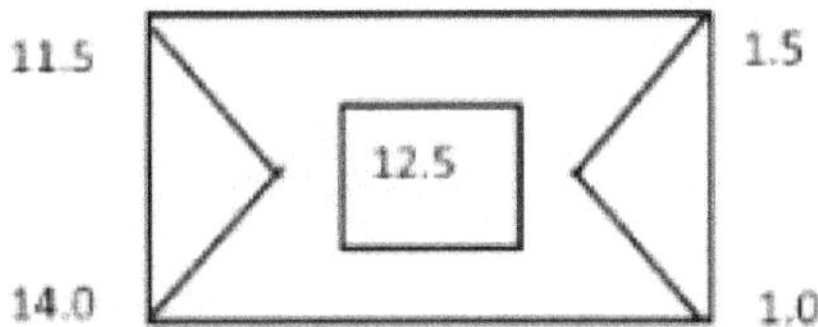

The home winemaker may not always have exact figures available. Therefore, estimations by trial and error are necessary. This is still desirable since one would like to enjoy his hard-earned wine bottle after bottle with the same degree of pleasure.

Color is often a problem in winemaking. It is often advisable to blend in at the crush a variety of red-colored juice, such as Rubired or Royalty. Alternatively, a small lot of wine of one of these varieties can be made to enhance the quality of the color. These two varieties are both excellent for blending since they impart little flavor.

Blending is also done between different ages of Sherry, known as solera sherry. It is done to produce a uniform product year after year.

Table of Wine Flavors and Aromas

Variety	Flavors	Aroma
White Wines		
Riesling	Fresh Apples	
Gewürztraminer	Spicy, Rose Petal, Peach, Lychee,	Honey Sweet Cabbage
Chardonnay	Rich Citrus (Lemon, Grapefruit) New Oak Barrels Adds A Buttery Tone	Mineral Or Mint
Sauvignon Blanc	Suggesting Bell Pepper Or Freshly Mown Grass, Apple,	Smokey Qualities
Muscat	Peach, Rose Petal, Spicy	Pungent Floral
Pinot Gris	Delicate Citrus And Fruity	Mildly Floral
Viognier	Orange, Fruity, Mint	Buttery, Vanilla
Pinot Blanc	Almond Apple	Buttery, Fruity Hazelnut
Red Wines		
Shiraz	Spicy, Blackcurrant	Musk, Earth Truffle
Merlot	Black-Cherry Herbal, Currant	Coconut, Oaky, Smoke
Pinot Noir	Cranberry, Cherry, Raspberry	Fruity, Cherry, Plum Strawberry
Zinfandel	Nectarine, Sour Raspberry, Cherry	Tutti-Frutti, Candy
Alicante Bouschet	Tienturier Adds Deep Red Color	

13. Bottling

The final episode in our winemaking drama is bottling the product. Before bottling wine, one should test a sample because it is the last opportunity for any manipulation to improve the quality of the wine. Checklist:

1) Is the wine the color you desire? If not, what can be done?

a) Too much color. A clarifying agent such as activated charcoal can reduce this.

b) Weak color. This can be improved by blending with a deeper-colored wine.

2) Clarity. Take a large, clean wine glass and fill it 1/2-3/4 full of wine. Grasp the glass by the stem, raise it toward a good source of light, and examine it for any turbidity. If there is a problem, add a firming agent and then rack the wine.

3) Acid content. Taste the wine. This is done by slowly sipping a small amount of wine into your mouth over your tongue at the same time, sucking in large quantities of air. Swirl the wine around your mouth for about 3-6 seconds, then spit it out and wash it with water.

a) If the wine is flat, add kosher tartaric acid or blend with a high-acid wine,

b) If the wine is too acidic for your taste, add a carefully calculated amount of calcium carbonate.

Once you have finished with all the final manipulations, your wine is ready to be bottled. The preferred method of bottling wine is to use cork plugs for a longer shelf life. Screw caps are easier to use, but allow too much air onto the wine, which causes the its oxidation.

How do you insert a cork in a bottle? The corks should be soaked in water with 75 ppm SO_2 until the corks soften and become pliable. There are many different corking devices for the home winemaker. All of the devices work on the same general principle. The wet cork must be squeezed through a hole directly connected to the mouth of the bottle but smaller in diameter. This is done by squeezing the cork through a V-shaped funnel, which causes the cork to be compressed. Corks must be wetted before use. Once the cork is in the mouth of the bottle, it expands, filling the space. The cork will maintain this excellent seal if it is kept wet. If the cork dries out, then air will penetrate the wine and cause oxidation. This is why all corked wine bottles should be kept lying down to allow constant contact between the wine and the cork. This keeps the cork wet enough to maintain a good seal and prevent air from entering.

VIII. THE EFFECT OF TEMPERATURE ON WINE PRODUCTION

Controlling temperature throughout the winemaking process is crucial for producing fine wines. Temperature plays a significant part in the ripening of the fruit and continues until it reaches the customer. The best quality grapes of the best varieties may not result in superior wines if the proper temperature control is not maintained throughout the entire wine-making process.

Temperature control is vital because:

a) High temperatures during fermentation (30-36°C) are detrimental to yeast and decrease their growth rate. Reduced growth slowed down the rate of fermentation, and at temperatures above 37°C, fermentation stops.

b) High fermentation temperatures increase the chances of Lactobacillus sp. contamination and developing detrimental and toxic yeast products.

c) At high temperatures, more alcohol is evaporated during fermentation, thus reducing the yield of alcohol/amount of sugar.

d) High fermentation temperatures decrease the aromas and flavors of white wines,

e) Excessive temperatures during storage induce a general instability in the wine.

f) If the temperature is too hot (>30°C) or too cold (<15°C) during the initial stage of the fermentation of red wines, then color and flavor extraction will decrease.

g) Low (<10°C) aging temperatures slow the aging process to an uneconomical point.

Below is a table that outlines the recommended temperature ranges for some of the wine-making processes.

Recommended Temperatures for Some Wine-making Processes

Temperature values are given in °C.

Type	Crush	Fermentation	Cellar
White Dry	13 -18	10 - 16	13 -18
Sweet	13 -18	10 - 16	13 - 18
Red Dry	13 - 14	18 - 29	13 - 18
Sweet	18 - 24	18 -29	13 –18
Red	21 – 32	21 – 30	15 - 21
White	21 – 32	21 – 28	15 –21
Sherry	21 - 32	21 – 29	15 –21
Sparkling*	——	10 – 15.5^	13 - 18

* Made from a blend of dry table wines

^ For the secondary fermentation, whether bottle or bulk.

Effect of Temperature on the Fruit

The ambient air temperature during ripening greatly affects grapes' chemical composition. To produce good wines, the fruit must be closely supervised before harvesting. In warm growing climates like Israel, there is a rapid change in the amount of organic acids and sugars during fruit maturation. Hot weather at the end of the season causes a rapid drop in total acid and an equally rapid increase in the sugar content. Alcohol yield is also affected by the accumulated heat during picking. Warmer years produce more alcohol per degree of must sugar.

The actual time of harvesting is also essential. Grapes in hot countries like Israel exposed to direct sunlight can reach temperatures above 60°C. Reducing this excess latent heat to proper fermenting temperatures would be far too expensive. Grapes should be harvested first thing in the morning to limit the amount of temperature modification the must require to reach proper fermenting temperatures.

The Effect of Temperature on Wine Quality.

The quality of white table wines is increased when the must is fermented to 10-16°C. With red wines, there is an optimum temperature for color and flavor extraction from the skins between 18-30°C. Low temperatures do not extract sufficient color; higher temperatures extract more color, but much of it is unstable. Temperatures above 50°C tend to pr-muse undesirable aromas, which have been described as horsey or barn-like. The total acidity is also affected by temperature. The maximum total titratable acid is achieved when the must is fermented between 2-27°C. Some of the other effects of temperature on the chemical composition of wine are:

Fermentation of red wines at high temperatures encourages malo-lactic fermentation during regular fermentation, thus lowering the total acid content.

The loss of aromas and alcohols increases with the increase in temperature and

Prolonged fermentation at low temperatures with high sugar increases the volatile acid content.

The quality of white wines, made from moldy grapes, improves if fermented at higher temperatures than usual. It is traditional to age sweet wines at warmer temperatures than table wines. Controlled heat treatments can produce flavors in dessert wines. Baked sherry requires prolonged heat (49-60°C) treatment (six weeks to months) depending on the "baked character desired. Superior flavor is achieved by baking at lower temperatures.

Temperature control during the secondary fermentation that produces sparkling wines is also important. The yeast starter used for the fermentation should be acclimated to the temperature and alcohol level prior to use. The best quality sparkling wines are fermented below 15.5°C. At low temperatures, the wines have a fruity aroma and cleaner taste. After fermentation, the bottles of sparkling wine should be stored at 13-15.5°C to allow controlled yeast autolysis. At warmer temperatures, undesirable flavors develop from the rapid degradation of the yeast. When served cold, sparkling wines maintain their level of CO_2 much longer.

IX. WINEMAKING

Table wines were traditionally intended for consumption at meals. As one learns more about wine, one finds that tradition plays an important role in the world of wine.

Dry White Table Wines:

With an understanding of the operations involved in winemaking, one can begin to deal with making specific wines. Only experienced home winemakers with all the proper equipment and conditions should attempt to make quality white wines at home. White wines are delicate. The two most challenging problems the home winemaker faces with white wines are:

1) The fermentation of these wines must be between

10- 16°C and

2) They are exceedingly susceptible to oxidation.

White table wines are preferred light in color, ranging from pale yellow to gold, fruity, and tart with a distinctive varietal flavor. This may be achieved by using good grapes of varieties with distinct flavors (see the table in the section on Grapes).

Step 1. Pick 5-15% of the grapes used at around 15° Brix three weeks early. The must will be high in acid, which can be a source of natural kosher tartaric acid for later blending. Treat this lot of wine exactly as the primary fermentation. This step is recommended for all wine you make unless you have a kosher commercial tartaric acid source.

Step 2. Prepare a pure wine yeast starter. It should be 3-5% of the total amount of grapes in your main fermentation. Use the same variety of grapes or one with a neutral taste to not interfere with the distinct flavor you are trying to achieve. It is essential to begin the starter neither too soon nor too late. When added to the main lot of must, it should be actively fermenting. The starter can be increased by about 1:10 every week.

Step 3. On the day you begin your primary fermentation, start all your procedures as early as possible in the morning. This will help keep the grapes and must at a low temperature. The grapes should be scrutinized, and all diseased berries should be removed. The grapes are then transferred from the picking bins to the vessel used for crushing (by hand, foot, or machine). Crush a random sample of berries and make your first analysis for acid, sugar, and pH. White wines should have at least 0.8% total acid as tartaric, and the must should range from 20-23" Brix. The grapes are then crushed, destemmed, SO_2 added, and immediately pressed. The clearer the must, the fruitier the taste is, but with a simple, uncomplicated flavor.

Cloudy musts produce wines with a more complex character. A comparison between clear vs. cloudy musts showed that the clear musts produced superior wines. Whether to ferment with a cloudy or clear must will depend on the type of character one wants in the wine. The complex hearty flavor is due to fusel oils alcohols with more than two carbons, which form due to air contact with the suspended colloids in the must. To achieve this flavor and body, they must be left in contact with the skin longer.

Chardonnay is the recommended variety for high-quality white wines. The maximum must-skin contact should not extend to 16 hours. The problem in this process is excessive exposure to air, which will cause damage due to oxidation. This can be solved by blanketing the must with inert gas (like nitrogen or carbon dioxide). This requires a gas source and air-tight containers to prevent leakage.

Step 4. Fermentation: Most white wines are fermented at 10-15°C. It takes 12-18 days to complete the active fermentation phase. When sugar is converted into ethanol, heat is given off. To control this increase in temperature and maintain the proper low temperatures for the white must to ferment, it is necessary to refrigerate. The lower the temperature, the slower the fermentation. At 1-3°C, the fermentation can take six months to finish. These long fermentations produce unique flavors and aromas, an essential criterion of a superior wine. At home, this isn't easy to achieve. The simplest way to centralize the temperature of the fermentation is to place the fermenting vessels in an air-conditioned room. Small lots (1-5 liters) can be fermented in your refrigerator at 4°C. Fill the bottle 1/2-3/4 full and place an airlock on it. Let the wine ferment during the day in the fridge and at night when the temperature is below 15°C. Allow the wine to ferment outside. This will speed up the fermentation, so it should not take longer than 6-9 weeks.

Step 5. Fermentation is concluded when no more bubbles are observed in the air lock for over 1/2 hour. Now, test the wine for total acid and pH. If the pH is low, i.e., less than 3.5, add 70-90 ppm SO_2. If the pH is higher, add acid if available and then add 90-12O ppm SO_2.

Several companies produce simple kits for testing the total acidity of wine. They are readily available via the Internet.

Step 6: Allow the wine to settle for 4-7 days, and then rack the wine off the lees. The upper third is clear, the middle third is slightly cloudy, and the bottom third next to the lees is the least clear. If possible, try to keep these fractions separate to facilitate later rackings. Remember after racking to keep all the vessels with wine filled to the brim and sealed to prevent oxidation,

Step 7. Clarify the wine with bentonite as it removes polymeric phenols and heat-labile proteins. Then, rack the wine of the bentonite complex after 15-25 days.

Step 8. Analyze the wine and make all corrections and adjustments.

Step 9. Make a final racking, if necessary, and blend if desired.

Step 10 Bottle. If you have kept lots separately during the fermentation, make sure to label them properly so you can compare the effects of your procedures on the final product.

White wines are best stored in a cool, dark environment. They are particularly sensitive to heat and sunlight.

Dry Red Table Wines

Step 1. Prepare starter.

Step 2. Pick grapes at 22-24° Brix. Cull for all diseased berries.

Step 3. Crush and destem the grapes.

Step 4. Add SO_2 at 8-120 ppm and wait for two hours.

Step 5. After two hours, add the starter.*

Step 6. Cap Management.

Red wines are fermented with the skins for the first week. Red pigment and much of the flavor are found in the skins of the grapes. Most grape juice is clear; therefore, making white wines from red varieties is possible. The longer the skins are kept in contact with the must, the more color will be obtained. As the must ferments, the rising amount of alcohol acts as an efficient solvent on the skins, releasing an increasing amount of color. For a rose wine, ferment with the skins for about three days. For a full red-colored table wine, ferment with the skins for 5-8 days, depending on the variety.

Fermentation gives off large amounts of heat. The skins in the must float to the top and form an insulating layer called a cap. The cap must be broken up and mixed with the fermenting must for two reasons. The first is to reduce the cap's insulating effect and to allow the built-up heat to escape. The second is to allow better contact between the fermenting must and the skins. This interaction allows for better extraction of color and flavor. The cap should be mixed back into the must 2-3 times daily. This can be accomplished without difficulty with a wood or plastic stick. Using any metals other than stainless steel causes heavy metal contamination. The fermentation would be maintained at room temperature, 20-28 °C.

Step 7. When the desired amount of color has been extracted from the skins, the skins, seeds, and other debris should be removed. Drain off as much of the must as possible. Then, sieve the remaining mixture through gauze. When you have gathered 1-3 kg of the cap in the gauze, press the mix by wringing it out. This procedure is messy, so be sure to:

* = Note: Disregard steps 4 and 5 for natural fermentation. Modify steps 3, 4, and 5 to ferment by maceration carbonique. The initial fermentation should take place in an open vessel to facilitate Cap management.

1) Wear old clothes or an apron,

2) Have something to throw the pomace away in and

3) Have plenty of water available for cleaning up.

Step 8. After another 6-10 days (depending on the variety and temperature of the fermentation), the fermentation rate will definitely slacken off. At this time, the must should be transferred to a sealed vessel with an airlock.

Step 9. After fermentation is completed, allow the wine to settle for 7-10 days and then rack.

Step 10. Analyze the wine for as many characteristics you have facilities for (either chemically or organoliptically). Carry out required adjustments and rack if necessary.

Step 11. Clarify the wine. If you want to use egg whites, whip them up before adding them to the wine. Blend the egg whites in the same manner as one would fold them into a cake batter. Allow the clarifying agent to settle for 10-18 days, then rack depending on how fast the material settles. Make sure you have sufficient vessels to put the clarified wine into so that all the vessels will be one hundred percent full.

Step 12. Aging: The aging of red wines fundamentally differs from that of white wines. Aging wines in wood are for red wines (except for Chardonnay). All full-colored red wines benefit from some aging in wood. The preferred wood for barrels in most wineries is oak. In various countries, other types of wood are used to a small degree (such as redwood in California). Since small (10-30 liters) oak barrels are expensive and difficult to find, most home winemakers do not age wine in them.

Partial substitutes have been experimented with. Oak chips or sawdust have been added to the wine. These cannot replace the aging in barrels, but they add some oak bouquet and flavor.

Step 13. After the initial six months of aging, wine should be tested every two to three months to determine whether it has reached the desired effect. This process can take as long as two years. Upon completion, check the wine for clarity.

Step 14. The wine is now ready for bottling, labeling, and, if desired, more aging in the bottle. Bottle aging can take 3-36 months. I recommend experimenting with different amounts of aging in the bottle and observing the differences in bouquet and flavor with time.

Sweet Wines

Home winemakers worldwide have used almost every variety available (or combinations) to make sweet wine. In many wine-producing countries, some varieties have been favored over others primarily because they can reach 26° Brix or more. For example, in France, the famous sauternes are made from Semillon and Sauvignon Blanc. In Hungary, Tokay is made from Furmint.

Sweet table wines typically have less than 14% alcohol and range from 5-11%.

Classification of Wine by Sugar Content

Wine type Sugar Content
Dry   >0-0.2%
*Mellow 0.3-0.55
Sweet   0.5-1.0%

*= At this sugar content, the wine is not sweet but softer and distinctly different from dry table wines.

To make sweet wine from grapes without adding sugar, one must allow the grapes to reach at least 26° Brix. Some home winemakers enable the grapes to partially raisin on the vine before picking them. This, however, adds a caramel odor and flavor to the wine, which is often undesirable.

By far, most sweet wines made at home are made with added sugar. The amount of sugar depends on individual tastes. It ranges from 1 kg sugar: 10 kg grapes to 1 kg sugar: 2 kg grapes. The majority of home winemakers add the sugar right after crushing. Most of these people are not concerned about the precise amount of residual Sugar there will be. However, a hydrometer or refractometer is needed if you want an accurate amount of sweetness. A hydrometer measures cylinder buoyancy depending on the amount of sugar in a fluid. It is a graduated glass with a weighted tail. It is placed into the must, and the amount of sugar is in the must. Sweet wines are easy to make or protect against microbial contamination at home.

It is difficult for the home winemaker to achieve slightly sweet wines with 0.5-2.0% sugar. These wines are susceptible to secondary fermentation and need sterile filtering or pasteurization to keep them for any time. Remember, every degree of Brix is converted into approximately 0.55% alcohol.

There are as many variations on procedures for making sweet wines as there are winemakers. Below are two variations on making technically sound sweet wines: natural fermentation and controlled fermentation.

Natural fermentation:

Step 1. Crush and destem.

Step 2a. If you are using grapes with high sugar content, don't plan to add any sugar. Allow the must to begin to ferment. This is not recommended for white wines.

Step 2b. If you plan to add sugar precisely, use a hydrometer or refractometer to determine the amount of sugar to add.

.

Step 3. Allow 2-4 days of skin contact for good color extraction since a slowly fermenting process must extract little color. Then press and continue the fermentation.

Controlled fermentation

Step 1. Crush and destem.

.

Step 2. Add 80-120 ppm SO2.

Step 3. If you don't plan to add any additional sugar, go to step 4. However, if you want a sweeter wine, follow the procedure in step 2 of natural fermentation.

Step 4. After waiting 2-3 hours, add an active pure wine yeast starter.

All the following steps are identical for both systems.

.

Step 5. Ferment both red and whites at low temperatures.

Step 6. Rack the wine during fermentation to reduce the yeast population.

Step 7. Add 1-2% alcohol during the fermentation. Since wine yeast stops fermenting at 14% alcohol, you will achieve this faster and leave more residual sugar.

.

Step 8. Termination of the fermentation: If large amounts of sugar are not added to the must to ensure that there will be residual sugar at the completion of fermentation, then the fermentation must be stopped artificially. This can be done by lowering the fermentation temperature, adding large amounts of SO2 (130-150 ppm), and then racking the wine soon after, to reduce the yeast population.

Step 9. Allow the wine to settle, and then rack. Repeat this once or twice more.

Step 10. Clarify and rack.

Step 11. Stabilization: The best method to maintain low levels of sugar in sweet wines is by sterile filtration and aseptic bottling. These processes are often beyond the capacity of your standard home winemaking operation. The next best procedure to prevent secondary fermentation is adding sorbic acid. It should be added at a rate of

0.5-0.08%. It should not exceed more than this because, at high concentrations, it causes undesirable odors.

Dessert and Appetizer Wines

Appetizer and Dessert wines have an alcohol content between 18% and 21%. Dessert wines have perceptible amounts of sugar, while appetizer wines are dry or slightly sweet. The higher levels of alcohol are achieved by adding brandy spirits before completing the fermentation. The addition of alcohol depends on the ° Brix of the fermenting must. The fermentation can be stopped at whatever percent of sugar is desired in the final product.

How much Brandy spirits to add?

The formula for determining the amount of brandy spirits to add

is: $(A \times a) + (B \times b) = (A+B) \times m$.

Where A = weight of wine.

a = % alcohol of the wine.

B = weight of brandy.

b =% alcohol of brandy.

m =% alcohol of the desired blend.

Example: You desire the final product to have 20% alcohol, and you have brandy at 50% alcohol. The weight of the wine is 40 kg, and its alcohol content is 13% then the amount of brandy needed to fortify the wine to 20% is:

$(40 \times 13) + (50 \times E) = (40 + B) \times 20$

.520 + 5OB =800 + 2OB

3OB = 280

B=9.3 kg of brandy.

Below is a table showing some white dessert wines' characteristics.

White Dessert Wines

.Type	Flavor	Color	Sugar
Muscatel	Distinct Muscat	Light Gold	5-8° Brix
Angelica	Fruity	Yellow-Golden	8-9° Brix
White Port	Light & Fruity	Very Light Color	6-7° Brix
Sweet Sherry			
Baked	Raisin or Baked	Pale Amber	0-2° Brix
Aged	Caramel	Dark Amber	4-6° Brix

Simple dessert winemaking will be discussed because of the great differences in making some of these wines, the duration of some of the processes, and the fact that some are rarely made at home. For further details, see The Technology of Wine Making, M.A. Amerine et al. (1972).

Production Methods of White Dessert Wines:

Step 1, Harvest the grapes at maximum ° Brix, but without raisins or shriveling, because raisined berries give another taste that is not typical to these types of wine.

Step 2. Crush, destem and add SO2 (100ppm).

Step 3. Drain and Press. This step is critical because the must is exposed to large quantities of air. This step should be done as quickly as possible.

Step 4. Add pure wine yeast starter and ferment at 10-14°C.

Step 5. Fortification of fermenting musts with brandy spirits. The must is fortified early in fermentation to ensure sufficient sugar remains. Below is a list of the necessary sugar content of the must to produce the desired

wine.

Angelica   18° Brix
Muscatel or White Port 16° Brix
Sweet Port   12° Brix

When wine spirits are added at 15° Brix to make 20% alcohol by volume, the new sugar content of the blend will be approximately 7° Brix. The high alcohol content protects the high sugar content against secondary fermentation.

Step 6. Adding alcohol stops the fermentation. The fortified wine is then allowed to settle for 2-4 days and then ranked to remove most of the yeast.

Step 7. Most dessert wines are clarified with bentonite at a rate of 60 gm/100 liters. Allow the wine to settle and rack,

Step 8. Test the resulting wine, make any corrections necessary, and rack again if the wine is turbid.

Step 9. Bottle. These wines can be kept for several years because of their high alcohol content. For red dessert wines, the procedure is the same except allow the must to ferment on the skins for 6-5 days. Then press the mixture to remove the skins, seeds, and stems. The fermentation of dessert wine should be carried out at 20-25°C.

Sparkling Wines

Sparkling wines are wines with excess carbon dioxide caused by a secondary fermentation or adding carbon dioxide gas. Producing sparkling wines is outside the scoop of most home winemakers. Just skilled and experienced winemakers should attempt this. It requires one to invest time, money, and equipment. This section will, therefore, not be one of practical procedures but for providing the reader with general information on producing sparkling wines. With this information, the reader will be far better equipped to understand and select better-quality wine.

Three processes can accomplish the induction of carbon dioxide into wine:

1) Carbonation: adding CO_2 gas under pressure at low temperatures into the wine.

2) Bottle fermentation-induced secondary yeast fermentation in special reinforced bottles and

3) Bulk fermentation: Induction of a secondary yeast fermentation in large tanks.

The carbonation process is precisely the same as carbonating any liquid, such as sodas and carbonated fruit juices. The base wines are standard bulk-produced wines. Carbonated wines are popular among beginners in wine appreciation. Several samples are sold here in Israel. Many of them are lower in alcohol (5-9%) and sweet, which adds to their popularity.

Bottle fermentation is a long, complex, and arduous hand process. First, prepare the Cuvee. The Cuvee is the base wine for the secondary fermentation and is made from a blend of wines. Blending is done to promote a base wine with the following attributes: low alcohol, high acid (0.65-0.753%), light color, and a clean fruity aroma. The carbon dioxide is produced by adding sugar and pure wine yeast starter into each bottle and capturing the CO_2 produced by the fermentation in the bottle. The desired and acceptable amount of pressure of CO_2 in sparkling wines is four atmospheres. To promote one atmosphere of pressure at 10°C, one needs to add four grams of sugar per liter.

Therefore, to produce the needed four atmospheres, one must add 16 gm of sugar/liter. The starter should be actively fermenting and added at the rate of 2-3%. The yeast should be a low-temperature, high-pressure tolerant, and heavy variety. The dead cells readily fall out of suspension to the bottom of the bottle. This mixture of wine, yeast, and sugar is known as triage.

Secondary fermentation takes 4-6 weeks to complete. Once the fermentation is completed, the wine is allowed to age on the yeast sediment for at least one year. The yeast's autolysis (disintegration of dead cells) provides additional desirable flavors (thought to be amino acids). This is one of the major differences between battle- and bulk-fermented sparkling wines.

To remove the yeast from the bottle, one must get the yeast to settle out next to the cork at the mouth of the bottle. To accomplish this, the bottles are maintained in racks upside down. The bottles are riddled regularly, i.e., turned right and left to loosen the yeast and cause them to settle at the mouth of the bottle. When riddling is completed, the bottle is `jolted' by being dropped lightly back into the rack to encourage the downward movement of the yeast.

The bottles are turned 1/8 of a turn every day. As they age, they are moved to racks with increasingly greater angles to ensure that all the yeast is next to the kettle's mouth.

There are three methods for removing yeast from the neck of the bottle, which is known as Disgorging:

The first method is the traditional method of quickly removing the cork with its lees and yeast while losing minimal amount of wine.

This is accomplished by freezing a small `plug' of wine next to the cork, where the yeast is located. The bottle is held at a 45° angle, and the cork and plug are removed. The bottles are immediately sealed temporarily. Since some of the wine is lost, additional wine must be added before final bottling. This is called dosage. It is also an opportunity to alter the sugar or alcohol content if desired. The wine is then permanently sealed and ready for consumption.

The Transfer Method: In the second system, the wine and yeast are collected from many bottles in a large tank. The dosage is then added. The wine is then filtered and bottled in the original or new bottles.

Metodo Martinotti Method or Bulk fermentation:

The Metodo Martinotti, a unique method created and patented by Italian Federico Martinotti (1860-1924) in 1895, is the second method. A Cuvee is blended and placed in a large tank, to which the exact proportions of sugar and yeast are added as in bottled fermented sparkling wines. The fermentation is carried out at 10-14°C for 2-4 weeks, with occasional stirring of the fermenting wine to prevent thick yeast deposits. The sparkling wine is then racked off and filtered into a finishing tank, which is stabilized for excess tartrates. The wine is cooled, causing the tartrates to fall out of the solution, and then transferred into the bottling tank. Here, the dosage is added, and the final steps involve sterile filtering the sparkling wine and bottling it.

Sparkling wine should be kept as cold as possible when transferred or bottled. To prevent oxidation and maintain the pressure of the carbon dioxide, the wine should be kept under a blanket of nitrogen gas.

X. FRUIT WINES

Making fruit wine is popular among home winemakers. Fruit wines are not referred to by varietal names like grapes but are identified by the fruit used to make the wine.

Numerous fruits and non-fruits are made into wine. This includes every fruit you can think of from strawberry, blueberry, kiwi, mango, etc. Wines are made from vegetables, tomatoes, rhubarb, watermelon, and even onions! Flowers such as dandelion, carnation, honeysuckle, rose hip, and so on are used to make wine.

The big difference between grape juice and other fruit juices is that grape juice has all the growth nutrients, vitamins, and energy sources required to sustain good yeast growth and, therefore, good fermentation of the sugar to alcohol.

In most cases, the percentage of alcohol in fruit wines is 5% unless nutrients and or sugar are added to encourage yeast growth. This section describes the fruit wine from available fruit in easy step-by-step procedures.

Apple Wine (Cider)

The preferable varieties for making apple cider should be varieties that have a good sugar-acid balance as to provide a good taste to the final product.

Step 1. Pick apples and store them for a few days to develop aroma.

Step 2. Wash and sort out all damaged and diseased apples.

Step 3. Crush and press the apples. Remove the seeds, as they have a bitter taste.

Step 4. Keeving: Cool the juice to 4-8°C and allow the juice to settle. The underlying principle is to remove nutrients from the juice by allowing the pectin to bind to them. This is done at the beginning of the process to ensure a long, slow fermentation. This allows the fermentation to reach a point where residual sugar remains. Most apple ciders are not fermented to the end and are preferred to be sweet to some extent. Keeving allows the cider to be bottled while still sweet and with no fear of excessive re-fermentation later.

Step 5. Sulfur Treatment: Add 50-100 ppm SO_2/liter.

Step 6. Check acidity. If below 0.6 gm/L than add lactic acid to increase the acidity.

Step 7. Fermentation: Fermentation can be carried out naturally, but better results are achieved by the addition of a pure wine yeast starter. Fermentation should be conducted cold (4-8°C). This can be done in small amounts in your refrigerator. Fermentation lasts 4-6 weeks. After initial fermentation, a secondary fermentation often occurs lasting between 4-6 weeks. Often apple wine undergoes a malo-lactic fermentation.

Step 8. When fermentation finishes, allow the wine to settle and then rack. Repeat this 2-3 times.

Step 9. Bottle.

The resulting wines are 5-6% alcohol. Dessert wines can be made by blending in neutral high alcohol spirits (see section on dessert wines).

Cherry Wine

Sour cherries are preferable to sweet cherries for making wine as the acidity of sweet cherries is too low. A blend of sweet and sour cherries can also be used. Crushed cherry pits add some additional flavor to the wine, but do not crush more than 8-10% of the pits because at high concentrations, they cause an undesirable flavor.

Step 1. Wash and sort out all damaged and spoiled cherries.

Step 2. Crush. Some people like to leave some cherries whole during the fermentation.

Step 3. Add 75-100 ppm SO_2.

Step 4. Wait 2 hours and add 2-5% actively fermenting pure wine yeast starter.

Step 5. Ferment in open containers at 15-20°C (cool room temperature) for 8-10 days and then press.

Step 6. Once the cherry must be fermenting less rapidly, transfer it to a closed container with an airlock.

7. After completion of fermentation allow the wine to settle and then rack.

8. If necessary, clarify with bent/unite and then rack.

9. Bottle.

Plum Wine

Step 1. Crush the plume and add 2 liters of water for every kg of fruit.

Step 2. Add 80-110 ppm SO_2/L.

Step 3 Wait 2-3 hours and add 3-5% actively fermenting pure wine yeast starter.

Step 4 Ferment at 20-25°C for 8-10 days and then press. Additional sugar can be added if desired. The amount will depend on whether a table or dessert wine is preferred. The wine should be now in a closed container with an airlock.

Step 5. After fermentation has finished, allow the wine to settle and rack. Rack again after it has settled for an additional two weeks.

Step 6 Analyze the wine for sugar and acid content. If the plum wine is low in acid, lactic or citric acid can be added to correct the total acid content. Plum table wine should not be below 0.6% total acid, and dessert wine should not be 0.5%.

Step 7 Clarify with bentonite and then rack.

Step 8. If dessert wine is desired, fortify now with neutral high-alcohol spirits to 20% alcohol. Remember that adding more liquid will lower the acid and sugar content per liter of wine. Therefore, consider this when doing Step 6.

Step 9. Bottle.

Pomegranate Wine.

Step 1. Do not crush, but press the whole fruit.

Step 2. Add sugar to reach 21-23° Brix.

Step 3. Add 70-100 ppm SO2 and wait 2-3 hours.

Step 4. Add 2-3% actively fermenting pure wine yeast starter.

Step 5. Ferment at 20-25°C for 8-12 days. When the fermentation has slowed down, transfer to the vessel with an airlock.

Step 6. Upon the completion of fermentation, allow the wine to settle and then rack. Repeat this procedure after 15-20 days.

Step 7. If a dessert wine is desired, fortify it to 20% alcohol and adjust its sugar and acid content.

Step 8. Bottle.

Honey Wine (Mead).

Mead has a comparatively high alcohol content compared to beer and table wines. Three essential ingredients are honey, yeast, and water. Since honey is the fundamental component, the resulting mead should have a very nice bouquet.

Mead is classified by the flavoring added to it. They are:

Traditional: mead is made with honey, water, and yeast.

Metheglin: mead made with added herbs or spices, such as cloves or cinnamon.

Melomel: mead made by adding fruit or fruit juice to traditional mead.

Cyser: mead made with apples or apple juice.

Pyment: mead made with grapes or grape juice.

Hipocras: is made from wine mixed with sugar and spices, usually including cinnamon, and possibly heated.

Sack: a more robust (higher alcohol content) mead made with a higher honey-to-water ratio.

There are many different flavored honeys available. Be sure to select one with a mild flavor. Honey from onion flowers will make wine difficult for some palates.

Step 1. In a large pot, dilute the honey with good-quality water at a rate of 1.5 kg to 4 liters, and then pour it into your primary fermenting vessel.

Step 2. Add K-meta-bisulfate at a rate of 80-100 ppm SO_2. This will kill the wild yeast, which cannot ferment your honey to a high alcohol percentage. Mix the solution well and let it sit for 24 hours.

Step 3. Check sugar concentration. Most people like to start around 22° Brix. Higher concentrations will produce a Sack mead.

Step 4. Hydrating Yeast: This should be done 15 minutes before the end of step 2. Warm 50 ml of water to 40 °C, and add the dry wine yeast. Mix thoroughly to break up any clumps, and let it sit for 15 minutes. Since this mixture has no nutrients for the yeast to grow, please don't leave it beyond the required time; the yeast will begin to die.

Step 5. Unlike grape juice, juice honey is deficient in the nutrients necessary for good yeast growth. Add yeast food, like (NH4)2O4, because honey lacks many elements needed for good growth. Add 14 gm (NH4)2HPO4, 1 gm potassium bitartrate (kosher brand), and 0.25 gm magnesium chloride or calcium chloride for each liter of diluted honey acid. These can be dissolved by heating them in a small amount of diluted honey and then stirring them into the main solution.

.

Step 6. Yeast. Now, add the hydrated yeast.

Step 7. Mead will take a long time to ferment. Fermentation times can be measured in months. Mead likes to ferment a little warmer than beer (23-28°C). Rack mead while it is fermenting. If you make any mead besides traditional, you must rack it about a week after removing the bits of fruit and spices that settle out. Rack periodically after that to get the mead off the dead yeast and other matter that settles out every 3-6 weeks, depending on the rate of fermentation and settling. This improves the flavor and clarifies the mead.

Initial fermentation of melomels made with fruit (not just juice) is most accessible in a food-grade plastic pail, where you can strain the fruit before racking. Glass carboys with fermentation locks are also the best fermentation vessels.

Step 8. Conduct an acid-sugar ratio evaluation and make adjustments.

Step 9. After the fermentation is complete (when there is less than one bubble per minute), allow the wine to settle out of the lees. At the end, clarify the mead and rack again. The wine can be preserved for periods of time, but it needs flash pasteurization.

Step 10. Bottle: Make sure all your equipment and bottles are clean.

XI. SENSORY EVALUATION

The sensory evaluation of wine is the analysis of wine by our senses of taste, sight, and smell. Wine evaluation is very subjective because physiological, psychological, and cultural factors greatly influence our sensory evaluation. Serious wine "tasters' try to eliminate as many of these factors by tasting wines blindly. A blind tasting means that the wine taster receives a sample without previous knowledge of its origin, type, producer, or age.

The aesthetic value of wine is one of the most critical and complex factors for the wine taster to evaluate. Different wines give varying degrees of pleasure to various individuals. The greater our knowledge of wine, the more competent we are at judging wines and the greater our capacity to enjoy a greater diversity of wines.

Our initial reaction to an aesthetic object like wine is subjective: We either like it or we don't. However, our evaluation and pleasure of wine is a learned response, based on our knowledge and sensory pleasure of wine. As we taste more wines, learn to identify varietal aromas and flavors, our appreciation of wine will increase, empowering us to enjoy a greater diversity of wines.

Many misnomers need to be elucidated concerning wines. Never depend on the reputation of a variety, name of a producer, area or origin, or price to judge the quality of a wine. In our modern world of high-pressure marketing, be careful not to be swayed by flashy labels or sexy advertisements. The single accurate test of any wine is a blind tasting. The intelligent wine connoisseur will depend on their accumulated knowledge and sensory perception of a wine and ignore the advertising agencies and wine experts.

A few other misnomers about wine that are not true should also be cleared up.

Wine judges are born into certain families. These are snobs. The skill to judge a wine is a learned skill. Only people with medical problems with their organoleptic facilities cannot judge wines.

Not only experts can fully enjoy the quality and characteristics of wines. The expert may understand why he enjoys a particular wine, but the pleasure derived from wine is individual and almost only subjective.

Well-known producers of wine do not always produce superior wines.

There are good years and not-so-good years. The wines of certain regions don't automatically make them superior to wines from other areas.

4) Not all wines improve with aging. White wines may improve to some extent after a few years; however, additional aging adds nothing. Excessive aging can easily lead to oxidation in white wines. Not all red wines need to be stored in wood. Excessive wood aging leads to an overpowering, oaky, or woody odor. Upon aging certain varietal wines, they will acquire nuances of bouquet that they lack as young wines. With excessive aging, red wines are also subject to oxidation and browning. To praise a wine because it is old and aged for a long time ignores its overall characteristics. This is a gross error a knowledgeable wine taster should never make.

5) Decanting red wines before serving does not always improve their quality. It is effective with wines that have some defect, such as excessive gassiness or an off odor that will evaporate before they are drunk. Decanting is more likely to improve a young wine than an old wine since the quality of old wines can deteriorate rapidly when exposed to air.

6) Never depend on the price of a wine as a guide to its quality. Prices are a matter of marketing. Also, if you equate price and quality together, you may find that some of the cheaper wines (though not the best) are a 'far better buy for the money.

9) This section will discuss using our senses in sensory evaluation.

Our sense of sight accounts for two aspects of wine evaluation: color and appearance. Vision is the sense we use first when evaluating a new wine. The color of the wine is the first thing we see. The evaluation of color is subjective, and its appreciation is learned over time. Some colors are more pleasing to the eye, such as a transparent bright red vs. a brown or a light yellow over dark amber. Our response to color seems to originate from an acquired knowledge of what color is appropriate for a particular wine type. People will enjoy a brown sherry but not a brown White Riesling. The color of wine is not static. The color of wine darkens with time. No white wine is truly white. They range from an under-ripe greenish tint to amber. The riper the grapes, the more pigment is found in the wine. White wine kept in wood casks or a bottle for a few years will turn amber or brown.

Rose wines should be pink with no brown, purple, or tawny tint. Most of the time, these tints show excessive aging or oxidation of the wine. A purple tint shows a high pH (low acid) wine. Low-acid wines are usually the result of excessive malo-lactic fermentation.

Most world wines are red, with a wide range of acceptable colors depending on the variety and age. Only teinturiers (red juiced varieties) will have a natural purple-red color. The desired color for most commercial wines is ruby red. Red wines that are bottle-aged develop an amber (or tawny) tint.

The tint (hue) and depth of color (lightness) tell us much about the condition of a wine. It can alert us to look for desirable or undesirable aromas and flavors. The third parameter of color is its purity. It takes experience and much learning to judge these three aspects of color. The human eye is most sensitive to the yellow-green region of the color spectrum. This makes judging the characteristics of red wines more complex than white wines. The apparent tint of a wine is also significantly modified by the color of the background and the source of the light.

Therefore, it is crucial to examine wines under a constant and adequate source of light. Fluorescent and mercury arc lamps can produce false tints in a wine. 'There is no perfect guide, but with experience, one learns to recognize the appropriate color and tint for each type of wine. It deficiencies can be due to the use of a high-pH wine, oxidation, excess metal content, and other wine disorders. High iron content in white wines causes a greenish-yellow tint, and in red wines, an iridescent film on the surface. With this information, never judge a wine in a dimly lit place such as a restaurant.

Below is a table outlining the wines that are preferred in different colors.

The Preferred Color of Different Wine Types.

Wine Type	Preferred Color
Table Wines	
White	
White Riesling	Greenish Yellow-Yellow
Chablis	Light Yellow
Chardonnay	Yellow-Light Gold
Sauvignon Blanc	Yellow-Light Gold
Red:	
Pinot Noir	Low-Medium Red
Petite Sarah	Low-Medium Red
Cabernet Sauvignon	Medium Red
Ruby Cabernet	Medium Red

Rosé: All Rosés Clear Pink

Sweet: Reds	Medium-Deep Red
Hock	Yellow-Light Gold
Sauternes	Yellow-Gold

Sherry:

Dry Baked	Light Amber
Sweet Baked	Medium Amber
Fino	Light Amber

Dessert:

White:

Muscatel	Light Amber-Gold
Port	Very Light

Red:

Tawny Port	Amber-Red

Ruby Port   Ruby Red

Champagne:

Red   Red

Rosé   Pink

White   Light Yellow

The appearance of a wine is judged on its clarity or freedom from suspended material, which is caused by poor winemaking practice, aging, which has left a deposit of dead yeast cells, and/or microbial spoilage.

Cloudiness is always a negative characteristic and a sign that one of the problems mentioned above exists.

Odor

Though color can be beautiful, it is an external affair. The most essential factor in the quality of a wine is its odor. It is more important than taste because of the unlimited variety of possible subtle differences. The olfactory nerve in our nose is responsible for our ability to sense different odors. Our sense of smell is susceptible to even trace amounts of aromatic substances. The olfactory nerve is a small region in the upper part of the nose. In the ordinary course of breathing, little air passes this region. Air must be diverted to the olfactory region to detect various aromatic compounds more accurately. This is done by sniffing. A good wine judge will learn to sniff well. People subject to colds or allergies are handicapped in this region. The most effective way of utilizing our olfactory nerve for wine evaluation is to place the nose into the glass above the wine and give a quick, forceful sniff; wait 15-50 seconds before repeating it not to fatigue the olfactory nerve.

Not all odors come to the olfactory region by breathing. Wine taken into the mouth warms up quickly, causing the evaporation of more aromatic compounds, which then move internally from the mouth to the olfactory region. These internally sensed odors are essential to the factors that make up what we call flavor.

Recent research has shown that the most critical aromatic compounds in wine are derived from chemicals called monoterpenes. These are found in two forms: bound and unbound. Unbound monoterpenes are very aromatic. A new natural enzyme has been found that releases the bound forms to unbound, increasing the natural aroma of the wine.

The desirable and pleasant odors of wine arise from four primary sources. They are:

1) The variety of the grape,

2) Byproducts of fermentation,

3) Treatments given to the wine during processing and

4) The aging process.

Odors originating from the grape itself are called aromas. Odors emanating from fermentation, processing, or aging are called bouquets. The table below lists different varieties and their characteristic aromas.

Wine Varieties and their Characteristic Aromas

VARIETY	AROMA
White Wines	
Muscat Alexander	Pronounced odor of floral linalool. Once recognized, easy to identify.
French Colombard	Mildly distinctive aroma. Overripe grapes give a powerful odor.
White Riesling	Fruity apple-like
Chardonnay	Fig-Apple-Melon aroma. Changes by aging in bottles or barrels from simple to very complex
Sauvignon Blanc	Distinctively spicy or weedy (herbaceous). It improves when grown in cool regions
Semillon	Different from Chardonnay, but still has the same fig-apple-melon aroma
Less & Non-Distinctive	
Burger, Syltanina, Chenin Blanc, Sylvanner	
Red Wines	
Muscat Hamburg Cabernet Sauvignon	Like Muscat Alexander floral linalool
Ruby Cabernet	Both are similar, strong aromatic-spicy aroma both in the grape and wine. Their aroma is compared to green olives or weeds (Cut grass, herbaceous.
Petite Sarah	Moderately distinctive with a complex aroma to describe. It has a fruity, ripe grape character.

Pinot noir

It is one of the most challenging and elusive. Aromas include roses, fruits, black cherry, berry, and currant. Its varietal aroma increases during the first years of aging.

Less & Non-distinctive

Carignane, Grenache, Gamay, Nebbiolo

See the appendix for a List of Wine Aroma Terminology

Bouquet:

All young wines have a yeasty fermentation bouquet. This yeasty bouquet lasts less than a year. Most wines lose this yeasty odor within a few months of bottle aging. Wines made by maceration carbonique retain this musty bouquet longer. It is not found to be agreeable to everyone.

There are several other essential odors imparted on wines during processing.

1) The baked bouquet of sherry or port (very distinct

caramel-like odor).

2) Sparkling wines which have been held on yeast

for extended periods of time, develop a very distinct bouquet,

3) Wines aged in wood (oak) add a desirable bouquet if not

overdone.

Aging in the bottle often causes a memorable bouquet, especially in red wines. It is easier to recognize than it is to describe. It is much more subtle than most of the other bouquets.

Foreign and Undesirable Odors:

One of the most severe problems with wines is foreign and undesirable odors. This includes off odors and odors that are not where they belong. For example, a recognizable woody odor in most white wines is a negative factor or a sherry's baked odor in a table wine is also highly undesirable.

A typical undesirable odor in white wines is that of sulfur dioxide. Sulfur dioxide is the smell of a burning match. It is a negative quality and repulsive to most people. Sulfur dioxide is found in white wines of low pH. Besides being an undesirable quality, it masks desirable odors. In high concentrations, it can cause sneezing and pain. Detectable SO_2 odor is a sign of poor winemaking practice.

Most of the remaining undesirable odors can be categorized by their source. They are:

a) From the grapes,

b) Due to fermentation and or later processing and

c) Due to microbial contamination.

Off-odors derived from the grape are earthy, green, raisiny, stemmy, and moldy. Earthiness is an off-odor found in specific areas. The earthy character is perceived after the wine has been in the mouth for a few seconds. Though commonly spoken of as an odor, is a mixed sensation and should be considered as a flavor. Tests have shown that it is not from the soil or the grapes but is thought to be caused by particular localized microflora on the grapes or the winery equipment. The green or leafy odor is caused by identifiable compounds (6-carbon alcohols and aldehydes). Grapes grown in cool climates or immature grapes can produce wines with this off-odor. The raisiny odor is easily recognized as the caramel odor. It is caused by the use of raisined grapes for winemaking.

The odor stemminess has just about disappeared with the almost universal use of crusher-destemmers. Anyone who has crushed grapes and smelled discarded stems can easily identify it. It is an herbaceous, cut grass odor.

Bad manufacturing practices cause many undesirable odors during the fermentation and processing of wine. These are baked, cooked, corked, fusel, hydrogen sulfide, mousy, oxidized, etc. The cooked odor is distinctly different from baked. It is caused by the wine being fermented at too high a temperature. This is still a prevalent problem throughout the world especially among white wines fermented above 25°C. As more wineries realize that cooling is necessary to make good white wine, this problem should disappear.

Corked is an undesirable odor that develops just in wines sealed with corks. It is found in both new and old wines. It is seen when porous corks are used. Most often, species of bacteria penetrate the cork's pores and start the cork's decay. It is not shared and, without difficulty, avoided. Bottles of wine suffering from this disorder have leaked through the cork. Therefore, avoid buying any wine that shows signs of leakage. This problem can be controlled by treating the corks with SO2 before use. At home, one can make a solution of 100 ppm SO2 and soak the dry corks before using them to seal bottles of wine.

Fusel odor is an easily identified and more prevalent problem in dessert wines. It is caused by multiple carbon alcohols called fusel oils. At high concentrations, it is unpleasant, but in small dosages, it adds character and complexity to a wine.

Hydrogen sulfide and mercaptans are detectable in minute amounts (two parts in a billion). It is the rotten egg smell. It is one of the most common foreign odors. They are produced from decaying yeast. The scent disappears after the first racking. There are several types of microorganisms that cause off-odors in wine. Most of them are wild yeast or bacteria. All these microorganisms attack organic compounds in the wine, such as tartaric acid, alcohol, sugar, glycerin, etc. They cause off-odors. These off-odors indicate other serious chemical imbalances in the wine. The cause of the musty odor in some wines has not yet been isolated. However, it seems to be associated with bacterial growth (actinomycetes). The microbial origin of the mousy odor is also in question. It is associated with wines with a high oxidation-reduction potential and oxidized wine.

Small amounts of acetic acid are produced by yeast during alcoholic fermentation. New wines range between O.02-0.03 gm of acetic acid/100 ml of wine. Higher concentrations result from contamination by one of the *Acetobacter* species. Acetic acid bacteria require large amounts of oxygen to grow and to oxidize ethanol to acetic acid. Acidification can be avoided by controlling the exposure to air.

The other major microbial disorder wine suffers from is lactic acid bacteria. Lactic acid bacteria cause a common problem known as malo-lactic fermentation. The bacteria convert malic acid to lactic acid, thus reducing the total titratable acid and causing a butter-like aroma. There has been an effort to standardize the wine aroma terminology in the past few years. The Sensory Evaluation Sub-committee of the American Society of Enology and Viticulture has proposed an exciting system. Their system is based on three levels of specificity, from general to specific. The figure on the next page shows the three-tiered wheel of wine aroma terminology they proposed.

Taste

In contrast to odor, taste is limited today to three basic sensations: sour or acid, hitter, and sweet. The sensation of taste is localized in special receptors on the tongue. Taste and flavor may begin together, but flavors are caused by compounds that once warmed up in the mouth. The olfactory nerve detects its aromatic natures. It is simple to check by comparing the taste and flavor of a wine when your nose is tightly sealed during a standard tasting.

Sweetness

The two primary factors for sweetness are glucose and fructose (two reducing sugars) and, to a limited extent by glycerol. The alcohol content of a wine modifies these. Ethanol enhances the apparent sweetness, while tannins reduce it. Fructose is the sweeter of the two sugars. Our ability to detect fructose is 35-50% greater than glucose, depending on their concentrations. For many people, sweetness masks or reduces the amount of sourness due to high acidity. Sweetness masks, to some extent, many other sensations such as astringency, bitterness, and vinegary. The sugar in sweet wines helps to appease our appetite, thus reducing the enjoyment and requirement for food to some extent. Hunger in humans is a function of sugar in the bloodstream. Dry table wines are preferred when eating a meal. It will thus add to the aesthetic pleasure of the food instead of reducing it.

Bitterness

Most people find the taste of bitterness unpleasant. Tannins, flavonoids, and other compounds cause bitterness. This is because white and rose wines have little tannin, and it is rare to find a bitter wine among them. However, full-bodied red wines are high in tannins and can have a bitter taste. Bitterness should not be confused with astringency. High astringency can mask bitter tastes. Not all bitterness is considered a negative trait. Some bitterness in red wines can be found to be a positive attribute.

Sourness

A sour taste is an essential and desirable part of the taste of wine. Wines lacking in acid have a flat taste. The acid: sugar ratio in all fruit is Crucial to the taste. Any fruit lacking sufficient acid will taste flat, which is considered a negative trait. The sourness of wine is a function of the total acidity and its pH. Sourness is affected by the sweetness of the wine, a person's saliva, the buffering capacity of the wine, and the balance of different organic acids present.

Wines with a pH of less than 3.1 or a total acidity of more than 0.9% will taste sour. Wines with a pH above 3.75 or a total acidity of less than 0.5% will taste flat. Tart, green, or unripe describe high-acid (sour) wines.

Different acids, in equal amounts, cause varying degrees of sourness. The sourness of the four essential organic acids found in wine, from the sourest to the least, are tartaric>citric>malic>lactic. The appropriate amount of acidity in a wine depends on the type of wine. White wines like Rieslings should be relatively high in acid, while sourness in sweet dessert wines gives the wine an unpleasant sweet-sour taste.

Touch

The feel, touch, or tactile sensations that wine gives us are important characteristics that allow us to appreciate the wine more. It is essential that one can distinguish between the sensations of taste and feel. The two critical features of the sensation of touch are astringency and viscosity. Astringency (puckery) is the sensation that causes our mouths and tongues to feel dried out. Astringency causes a stern, terse contraction or compression of soft organic tissue. It is a sensation of feeling distinguished from bitterness, a sensation of taste. Astringency in wines is caused by tannins (polyphenolic compounds). Astringency tends to mask bitterness, and the astringency in young wines decreases with aging. Viscosity is the amount or degree to which a liquid is fluid. The term "body' is often used synonymously with viscosity. The more viscous a liquid is, the more body it has. The body or viscosity of wine is primarily due to the ethanol and sugar content and is only minimally affected by glycerol. Glycerol is a much more viscous compound, but it is found in low levels in wine.

It is easy to check for the body of a wine and its alcohol content. Fill a Clear wine glass 1/2-2/3 full with wine. Next, swirl the wine around the glass and set it down. Above the present level of the wine, you will observe a small amount of wine dripping down the glass in tear shapes. The size and length of time it takes the tears to flow back into the wine's main body indicates the wine's viscosity. The larger the tears and the slower they move, the greater the viscosity and the higher the amount of alcohol.

Temperature

'There are two reasons temperatures are essential in the sensory evaluation of wines. First, the sensation of warm or cold in themselves is critical. Second, the effect of temperature on our other senses can alter our judgment of a wine. A warm white wine is less pleasing than a wine served cold; sparkling wines also maintain their gassiness better when kept at low temperatures. Low temperatures also lower compounds' volatility, making high SO_2 wines less repellant. Aromatic compounds will be more active and more straightforward to identify when a wine is served warm.

There are as many different systems for scoring wines as stars in the sky. Everyone has their particular system, some based on numerical values for various characteristics and some based on verbal or written evaluation. I prefer to use the scoring system developed at the University of California at Davis. It covers all the essential qualities of wine and leaves flexibility. This allows for some of the subjective preferences to be included in the grade of the wine. This enables one to value a wine based on its general quality. Researchers found that concentrating only on the wines' characteristics does not add up to a realistic picture of the wine's accurate evaluation. This portion of the test enables one to round out the wine's quality. The system is based on numerical characteristics. The total possible numerical score a wine can receive is 20 points. Wines with a score between 20-17 are superior wines. Wines that have no outstanding merit or defect are scored 13-16. Wines having scores of 9-12 are wines with some defect, but still commercially acceptable scoring is given in the following manner:

Numerical Evaluation

Appearance	Cloudy =0, clear=1 brilliant =2
Color	Distinctly off=0, slightly off=1 correct=2
Aroma & Bouquet	Vinous=1, distinct but not varietal=2 varietal=3
Vinegary	Obvious=0, slight=1. none=2/ Subtract 1 or 2 points for off odors. Add 1 point for a bottle bouquet
Total Acidity	Distinctly low or high=0, slightly low or high=1, correct=2
Sweetness	Too high or low=0, correct=1
Body	Too high or low=0, correct=1
Flavor	Distinctly abnormal=0, slightly abnormal=1, correct=2
Bitterness	High=0, slightly high=1, correct=2
General Quality	Lacking=0, slight=1, impressive=2

XII. SANITATION

Sanitation is not the same thing as cleaning or sterilization. To sanitize something is to reduce or remove bacteria and other undesirable microorganisms via heat or chemical means. Cleaning is the removal of visible dirt and residue from your equipment. Sterilization is the killing of germs, insects, or worms.

If your latest attempt at winemaking was less than satisfactory, look no further than the area where you made your wine. It is known that 90% of winemaking failures can be traced back to poor equipment sanitation standards and the production area.

Sanitation plays a vital role in winemaking. It is essential for the quality of the wine and the health of the people making the wine. All the equipment used in winemaking should be kept clean to prevent microbial contamination and off-tastes, aromas, and flavors. Before any equipment is used, it should be checked to see if it is spotless. Foreign materials can contribute to the reduction of the quality of the wine or, worse, be toxic. Clean all equipment well and use plenty of water to wash away any residue of the cleaning agents.

The area in which you work should also be kept clean to prevent accidents (such as slipping on wet garbage left around) and to prevent microbial contamination. There should always be a good water source close at hand for cleaning up. Garbage disposal is also important. Moldy unused grapes, pumice, or less left around will attract insects and possibly rodents. Always have garbage pails and bags available for immediate cleanup.

Sanitation during bottling is essential to prevent spoilage in the bottle. Finishing this long process and then spoiling the wine in the bottle would be a real shame. Treat the corks with SO_2 before use and clean the bottles with proper cleaning agents. Use sterile boiled water (boil the water for 20 minutes) to make the final rinse of the bottles before filling. This should be done immediately before bottling to ensure the bottles are as clean as possible.

Below is a table providing a partial list of the different cleaning and disinfecting agents that can be used.

Cleaning and Disinfecting Agents

Cleaning agents for plastic or glassware

Boiling water

Tri-sodium phosphate

Potassium Meta-bi-sulfite

Soda Ash

hydrogen peroxide

For cleaning wood or concrete

Tri-sodium phosphate

Sodium bicarbonate

Soda Ash

Boiling water

Chlorine

hydrogen peroxide

For Metal Equipment

Any of the materials for cleaning wood

Citric Acid

Abrasive carbon

For Sterilizing

Sodium or calcium hypochlorite

Sulfur dioxide

For Outside- Wood or Concrete

Lime

Sodium or calcium hypochlorite

Sodium Bisulfate

After the use of any of these cleaning agents, the equipment must be rinsed thoroughly with plenty of water.

The last step in our long procedure: לחיים!!!

XIII. WINE STORAGE AT HOME

The Importance of Proper Wine Storage

A delicate beverage, wine relies on your careful storage to maintain its quality and flavor. Your role in this process is crucial, whether for your everyday wines or your cherished collectibles.

Factors Affecting Wine Quality

Temperature: The most critical factor in wine storage. The ideal temperature is around 55°F (13°C) for all types of wine.

Too hot: Can cause "maderization," the turning of wine into vinegar

Too cold: This may cause the wine to expand, potentially forcing out the cork

Humidity: The optimal range is 50-80%.

Too dry: Corks can shrivel, leading to premature oxidation

Too humid: Can promote mold growth and damage labels

Light: UV rays can break down tannins, affecting wine structure and flavor.

Store wine in dark bottles or away from light sources

Position: Minimize movement and store bottles horizontally.

Reduces vibration that can alter wine's molecular structure

Keeps corks moist, preventing oxygen from entering the bottle

Odors: Wine can absorb surrounding odors through the cork.

Avoid storing near strong-smelling items

Storing Everyday Wines

For wines meant to be consumed young:

Keep in a dark, cool place with some humidity

A closet, pantry, or countertop away from heat sources works well

The refrigerator is suitable for short-term storage (a few days)

Wine coolers can provide ideal conditions if available

Storing Opened Wine

To preserve opened wine:

Recork immediately after pouring

Consider using a vacuum pump to remove air

Store in the refrigerator to slow oxidation

Long-Term Wine Storage

For aging wines or building a collection:

Wine refrigerators offer controlled temperature and humidity

Wine racks provide organized storage and display options

If no cellar is available, recreate cellar conditions:

Choose a cool, dark, and slightly damp location

Use a basement, garage, or cupboard (if odor-free)

Store bottles on their sides to keep corks moist

Protect from light, possibly using a blanket cover

Remember, opening a wine slightly earlier than too late is better. Don't hesitate to enjoy your special bottles.By following these guidelines, you can ensure your wines remain in optimal condition, whether you're storing them for a few days or several years.

APPENDIX I

142

List of Aroma and Taste Terminology

Taste, in contrast to odor, is limited today to three basic sensations; sour or acid, bitter and sweet. The sensation of taste is localized in special receptors on the tongue. Taste and flavor may begin together, but compounds that, once warmed up in the mouth, cause flavors. The olfactory nerve detects their aromatic natures. It is simple to check by comparing the taste and flavor of a wine when your nose is tightly sealed during a normal tasting.

The two primary factors for sweetness are glucose and fructose (two reducing sugars) and to a limited extent by glycerol. The alcohol content of a wine modifies these. Ethanol enhances the apparent sweetness, while tannins reduce it. Fructose is the sweeter of the two sugars. Our ability to detect fructose is 35-50% greater than glucose, depending on their concentrations. For many people, sweetness masks or reduces the amount of sourness due to high acidity. Sweetness masks to some extent many other sensations such as astringency, bitterness and vinegariness. The sugar in sweet wines helps to appease our appetite, thus reducing to some extent the enjoyment and requirement for food. Hunger in humans is a function of the amount of sugar in the blood stream. Dry table wines are preferred when eating a meal. It will thus add to our aesthetic pleasure of the food instead of reducing it

acetic: All wines contain amounts of acidity due to acetic acid. It is what gives it the vinegary smell. In excessive amounts, the wine will have a vinegary smell, essentially wine vinegar.

acidic: Wines need natural acidity to taste fresh and lively. Excessive amounts of acidity results in a wine that is tart and sour.

acidity, a critical component of a wine's quality, is a balance of citric, tartaric, malic, and lactic acids. Wines from hot areas tend to have lower acidity, while those from cooler regions have higher acidity. The right amount of acidity can preserve a wine's freshness and keep it lively, but too much can overpower the wine's flavors and texture.

aftertaste: The taste left in one's mouth after swallowing the wine is the aftertaste. It is a synonym for length or finish. The longer the aftertaste lingers in the mouth, the higher the quality of the wine.

aggressive: Aggressive is applied to wines that are high in acidity or harsh tannins or both.

aroma: Aroma is the smell of a young wine before it has had sufficient time to develop nuances of smell that are then called its bouquet. The word aroma is used to mean the smell of a relatively young, unevolved wine.

astringent: Astringent wines are not necessarily bad or good wines. Astringent wines are harsh and coarse to taste because they are too young and tannic and need time to develop or are poorly made. A wine's level of tannins (if it is harsh) contributes to its degree of astringency. It is the sensation that your mouth is dried out or puckered, like eating an unripe persimmon.

balance: One of the most desired characteristics in a wine is good balance. That is where the concentration of fruit, level of tannins, and acidity are in total harmony. Balanced wines are symmetrical and improve with age.

berrylike: Most red wines have an intense berry fruit character that can suggest blackberries, raspberries, black cherries, mulberries, or even strawberries and cranberries.

bitterness: Most people find the taste of bitterness unpleasant. Tannins, flavonoids, and other organic compounds cause bitterness. Since white and rosé wines have little tannin, it is rare to find a bitter wine among them. However, full-bodied red wines are high in tannins and can have a bitter taste. Bitterness should not be confused with astringency.

blackcurrant: A pronounced smell of blackcurrant fruit. It can vary in intensity from faint to deep and rich.

body: The body is the weight or viscosity of a wine that can be sensed as it crosses the palate. It is expressed as full-bodied, medium-bodied or medium-weight, or light-bodied. It is an easy procedure to check the body and alcohol content of a wine. Fill a clear wine glass half to two-thirds full with wine. Then, swirl the wine around the glass and set it down. Above the present level of the wine, you will observe a small amount of wine dripping down the glass in tear-shaped structures. The size and length of time it takes the tears to flow back into the wine's main body indicates the wine's viscosity. The larger the tears and the slower they move, the greater the viscosity and the higher the amount of alcohol.

***Botrytis cinerea*:** This fungus attacks the grape skins under specific climatic conditions (moist and warm weather). It causes the grape to become super-concentrated because it causes a natural dehydration. Botrytis cinerea is essential for the great sweet white wines of Barsac and Sauternes.

bouquet: As a wine's aroma develops from bottle aging, it is transformed into a bouquet that is hopefully more than just the smell of the grape.

brawny: A full-bodied wine with ample weight and flavor, although not always the most elegant or refined wine.

briery: I think of California Zinfandel when the term briery comes into play, signifying the wine is aggressive and rather spicy.

brilliant: Brilliant relates to the color of the wine. A brilliant wine is one that is clear, with no haze or cloudiness to the color.

browning: As red wines age, their color changes from ruby/purple to dark ruby, to medium ruby, to ruby with an amber edge, to ruby with a brown edge. When a wine is browning, it is mature and will not improve any more.

cedar: Red wines can have either a bouquet that faintly or overtly suggests the smell of cedar wood. The scent of cedar is a complex aspect of the bouquet.

chewy: If a wine has a relatively dense, viscous texture from a high glycerin content, it is often referred to as being chewy. High-extract wines from great vintages can usually be chewy because they have higher alcohol hence high levels of glycerin, which imparts a fleshy feel to the mouth.

Closed: The term closed denotes that the wine is not showing its full potential because it is too young. Young wines often close up about 12-18 months after bottling and, depending on the vintage and storage conditions, remain in such a state for several years to more than a decade.

complex: One of the most subjective descriptive terms used, a complex wine is a wine that the taster never gets bored with and finds enjoyable to drink. Complex wines have a variety of subtle scents and flavors that hold one's interest in the wine.

concentrated: Fine wines, whether they are light, medium, or full-bodied, should have concentrated flavors. Concentrated denotes that the wine has a depth and richness of fruit that gives it appeal and interest. Deep is a synonym for concentrated.

corked: A corked wine is a flawed wine that has taken on the smell of cork because of an unclean or faulty cork. It has a smell similar to wet cardboard.

cuvée: Many producers in the Rhône Valley produce unique, deluxe lots of wine or much wine from a specific grape variety they bottle separately. These lots are often referred to as cuvées.

deep: Essentially the same as concentrated, indicating the wine is rich, full of extract, and mouth-filling.

delicate: As this word implies, delicate wines are light, subtle, understated wines that are prized for their shyness rather than for an extroverted, robust character. White wines are more delicate than red wines. Few Rhône red wines can correctly be called delicate.

diffuse: Wines that smell and taste unstructured and unfocused are said to be diffuse. When red wines are served at too warm, they become diffused.

Earthy: It may be used in both a negative and a positive sense; however, I prefer to use earthy to denote a positive aroma of fresh, rich, clean soil. Earthy is a more intense smell than woody or truffle scents.

elegant: Although more white wines than red are described as being elegant, lighter-styled, graceful, balanced red wines can be elegant.

exuberant: As with extroverted, somewhat hyper people, wines too can gush with fruit and seem nervous and intensely vigorous.

floral: Wines made from the Muscat grapes have a flowery component, and red wine occasionally has a floral scent.

focused: A fine wine's bouquet and flavor should be focused. Focused means that the scents, aromas, and flavors are precise and clearly delineated. If they are not, the wine is like an out-of-focus picture: diffuse, hazy, and problematic.

forward: An adjective used to describe wines that are (1) delicious, evolved, and close to maturity, (2) wines that border on being flamboyant or ostentatious, or (3) unusually evolved and/or quickly maturing wines.

fresh: Freshness in both young and old wines is a welcome and pleasing component. A wine is said to be fresh when it is lively and cleanly made. The opposite of fresh is stale.

fruity: A superb wine should have enough concentration of fruit so it can be said to be fruity. The best wines will have more than just a fruity personality.

full-bodied: Wines rich in extract, alcohol, and glycerin are full-bodied wines.

green: Green wines are made from unripe grapes; they lack the taste and aroma of their varietal character.

Hard: Hard wines have abrasive, astringent tannins or high acidity. Young red wine vintages can be hard, but they should never be harsh.

harsh: If a wine is too hard it is said to be harsh. Harshness in a wine, young or old, is a flaw.

herbaceous: Many wines have a distinctive herbal smell that is said to be herbaceous. Specific herbal smells can be of thyme, lavender, rosemary, oregano, fennel, or basil. Cabernet Sauvignon has a distinct herbaceous taste when young.

hollow: Also known as shallow, hollow wines are diluted and lack depth and concentration.

hot: Rather than meaning that the temperature of the wine is too warm to drink, hot denotes that the wine is too high in alcohol and, therefore, leaves a burning sensation in the back of the throat when swallowed. Wines with alcohol levels over 14.5% often taste hot if the requisite depth of fruit is not present.

intensity: Intensity is one of the most desirable traits of a high-quality wine. Wines of great intensity must also have balance. They should never be heavy or cloying. Intensely concentrated great wines are alive, vibrant, aromatic, layered, and texturally compelling. Their intensity adds to their character rather than detracts from it.

leafy: A leafy character in a wine is similar to an herbaceous character because it refers to the smell of leaves rather than herbs. A wine that is too leafy is vegetal or green.

lean: Lean wines are slim, instead streamlined wines that lack generosity and fatness but can still be enjoyable and pleasant.

lively: A synonym for fresh or exuberant, a lively wine is usually a young wine with good acidity and a thirst-quenching personality.

long: a desirable trait in any fine wine is that it be extended in the mouth. Long, or length, relates to a wine's finish, meaning that after you swallow the wine, you sense its presence for a long time. Thirty seconds to several minutes is a great length. In a young wine, the difference between something good and something great is the length of the wine.

lush: Lush wines are velvety, soft, richly fruity, concentrated, and fat wines. A lush wine can never be an astringent or hard wine.

musty: Wines aged in dirty barrels, poorly maintained cellars, or exposed to a bad cork take on a damp, musty character that is a flaw.

nose: The general smell and aroma of a wine as sensed through one's nose and olfactory senses is often called the wine's nose.

oaky: Many red wines are aged from 6 to 30 months in various sizes of oak barrels. New oak barrels impart the wine a toasty, vanillin flavor and smell. If the wine is not rich and concentrated, the barrels can overwhelm it, making it taste overly oaky. The wine is rich and concentrated, and the winemaker has made judicious use of barrels; however, the results are a wonderful marriage of fruit and oak.

off: If a wine is not showing its true character or is flawed or spoiled, it is said to be "off."

overripe: An undesirable characteristic; grapes left too long on the vine become too ripe, lose their acidity, and produce heavy wines that lack balance. This can happen in the hot viticultural areas if the growers harvest too late.

oxidized: If a wine has been excessively exposed to air during either its making or aging, the wine loses freshness and takes on a stale, old smell and taste. Such a wine is said to be oxidized.

perfumed: This term applies more to fragrant, aromatic white wines than red ones. However, some dry white wines (particularly Condrieu) and sweet white wines can have a strong perfumed smell.

plummy: Rich, concentrated wines can often smell and taste like ripe plums. When they do, the term plummy is applicable.

precocious: Wines that mature quickly are precocious. However, the term also applies to wines that may last and evolve gracefully over a long period but taste as if they are aging quickly because of their tastiness and soft, early charms.

raisin-like: Late-harvest wines that are drunk at the end of a meal can often have a somewhat raisin-like flavor, which in some Ports and Sherries is desirable. However, a raisin-like quality is a major flaw in a dinner wine.

rich: Wines high in extract, flavor, and intensity of fruit flavor.

ripe: A wine is ripe when its grapes have reached the optimum level of maturity. Immature grapes produce under-ripe wines, and too-mature grapes produce overripe wines.

round: A desirable characteristic of wines, roundness occurs in mature wines that have lost their youthful, astringent tannins and in young wines with soft tannins and low acidity.

shallow: A weak, feeble, watery, or diluted wine lacking concentration is considered shallow.

sharp: An undesirable trait, sharp wines are bitter and unpleasant with hard, pointed edges.

silky: A synonym for velvety or lush, silky wines are soft, sometimes fat, but never hard or angular.

smoky: Some wines, because of the soil or because of the barrels used to age the wine, have a distinctive smoky character

soft: A soft wine is round and fruity, low in acidity, and has an absence of aggressive, hard tannins.

sourness: The sour taste is an essential and desirable component of the taste of a wine. The lack of acid in wines causes them to have a flat taste. The acid: sugar ratio in all fruit is crucial to the taste. Any fruit that is lacking in sufficient acid will be flat in taste, and it is considered a negative trait. The sourness of a wine is a function of the total acidity and pH. Wines with a pH of less than 3.1 or a total acidity of more than 0.9% will taste sour. Wines with a pH above 3.75 or a total acidity less than 0.5% will taste flat (insipid). Tart, green, or unripe describe high-acid (sour) wines.

spicy: Wines often smell spicy with aromas of pepper, cinnamon, and other well-known spices. These pungent aromas are lumped together and called spicy.

supple: A supple wine is one that is soft, lush, velvety, round and tasty. It is a desirable characteristic because it suggests that the wine is harmonious.

tannic: The tannins of a wine are extracted from the grape skins and stems. Along with a wine's acidity and alcohol content, tannin is essential to the wine's history. Tannins give a wine firmness and some roughness when young, but the roughness dissipates with time. A tannic wine is young and unready to drink.

tart: Sharp, acidic, under-aged wines are called tart. A wine that is tart is not pleasant to drink.

temperature: There are two reasons temperature is essential in the sensory evaluation of wines. First, the sensation of warm or cold in themselves, and second the effect of temperature on the other senses, which might influence our judgment. A warm white wine is found less pleasing than the same wine served cold. Sparkling wines also maintain their gassiness better when kept at low temperatures. Low temperatures also lower the volatility of compounds. This would make high SO_2 wines less repellant. Aromatic compounds will be more active and easier to identify, when a wine is served warm.

velvety: A textural description and synonym for lush or silky, a velvety wine is a rich, soft, smooth wine to taste. It is a desirable characteristic.

viscous: Viscous wines are concentrated, fat, almost thick wines with a great density of fruit extract, plenty of glycerin, and high alcohol content. If they have balanced acidity, they can be flavorful and exciting wines. If they lack acidity, they are often flabby and heavy.

volatile: A volatile wine smells of vinegar because of an excessive amount of acetic bacteria present. It is a seriously flawed wine.

woody: When a wine is overly oaky, it is often said to be woody. Oakiness in a wine's bouquet and taste is good up to a point. Once past that point, the wine is woody, and excessive oak aging masks its fruity qualities.

Below is the popular wine aroma wheel developed by Prof. A. Noble (1984, 1987) at the University of California at Davis.

Figure 11. Aroma Wheel.

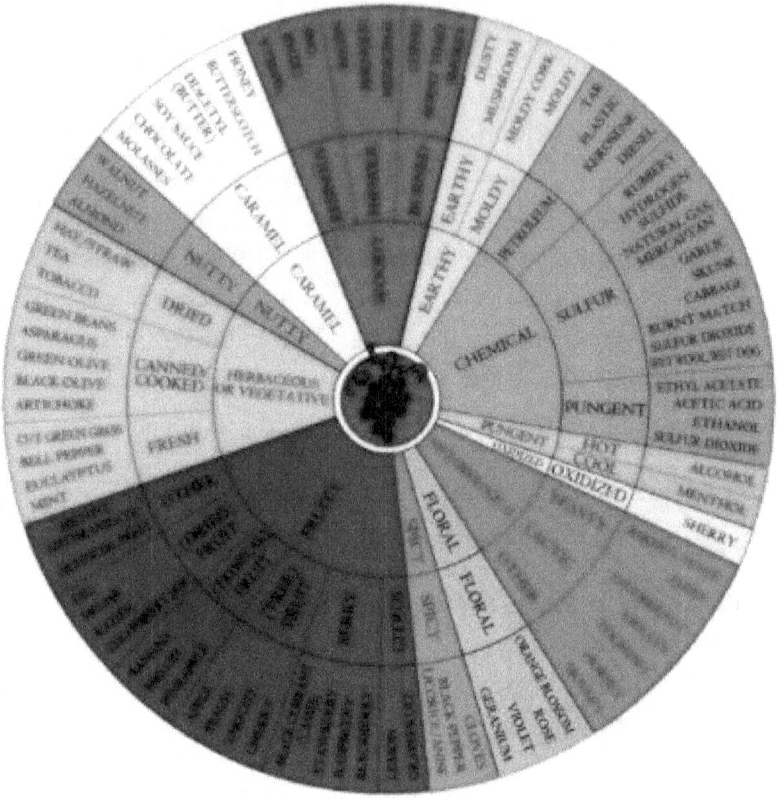
CHEMICAL
SULFUR
PUNGENT
PETROLEUM
EARTHY
MOLDY
CARAMEL
NUTTY
DRIED
CANNED/
COOKED
HERBACEOUS
OR VEGETATIVE
FRESH
FLORAL
SPICY
OXIDIZED
HOT
COOL
SHERRY
HONEY
BUTTERSCOTCH
DIACETYL
(BUTTER)
SOY SAUCE
CHOCOLATE
MOLASSES
WALNUT
HAZELNUT
ALMOND
HAY/STRAW
TEA
TOBACCO
GREEN BEANS
ASPARAGUS
GREEN OLIVE
BLACK OLIVE
ARTICHOKE
CUT GREEN GRASS
BELL PEPPER
EUCALYPTUS
MINT
DUSTY
MUSHROOM
MOLDY CORK
MOLDY
TAR
PLASTIC
KEROSENE
DIESEL
RUBBERY
HYDROGEN
SULFIDE
NATURAL GAS
MERCAPTAN
GARLIC
SKUNK
CABBAGE
BURNT MATCH
SULFUR DIOXIDE
ETHYL ACETATE
ACETIC ACID
ETHANOL
SULFUR DIOXIDE
ALCOHOL
MENTHOL
ORANGE BLOSSOM
ROSE
VIOLET
GERANIUM
CLOVES
BLACK PEPPER
LICORICE/ANISE

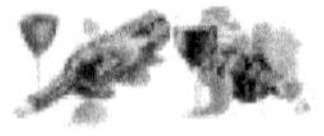

APPENDIX II

Table of Wine Additives

Additives	Function
Activated Charcoal:	to assist precipitation during fermentation to clarify-purify wine. to remove excess color in white wines.
Bentonite	To clarify wine
Calcium Carbonate:	to reduce excess acid
Casein	To clarify wines
Di-ammonium Hydrogen Phosphate (NH4)'2HPO4	Yeast food to aid in the difficult fermentation of products like fruit and honey wine.
Egg Whites	To clarify wines
Fumaric acid	Antiseptic, to prevent malo-lactic fermentation, it also adds to the total acidity.
Gum Arabic	to clarify and stabilize wine
Lactic acid	to add acid to fruit wines
Malic acid	to increase total acidity of wine
Oak chips	to simulate aging in oak barrels
Potassium (or Sodium) meta-bisulfate	to prevent oxidation antiseptic to kill wild yeast before initiation of fermentation
Sorbic Acid	Antiseptic and preservative Inhibits malo-lactic fermentation
Tannin	Aids in the clarification of wine
Tartaric acid	Increases total acidity of wine

APPENDIX III

List of Equipment and Chemicals

Fermenting and Processing

1. Airlocks

2. Bottles-many of all sizes

3. Crushing vat: Wood, stainless steel, plastic

4. Fermenting Vessels: Glass jars, food-grade plastic

    containers, stainless steel,

Water-proof wood barrels

5. Funnels

6. Hosing, tubing: Polyethylene, Teflon, silicon, stainless

    steel

7. Hydrometer

8. Press: Gauze cloth, mechanical

9, Refractometer

10. Stick for mixing cap

11. Thermometer

Wine and Must Analysis

1. pH-Litmus paper

2. Sugar -refractometer or hydrometer

3. Kit for testing for total acid

Fining and Clarifying Agents

1. Bentonite

2. Casein

3. Egg whites

4. Kosher gelatin

5. Charcoal

Bottling

1. Bottling

2. Corks

3. Corking device

4. Seals

Sanitation

1. Antiseptic-SO_2

2. Detergent

3. Garbage pails and bags

4. Soda Ash

5. Sodium meta-bisulfate

6. Sodium Carbonate

7. Sodium hypochlorite (bleach)

8. Water hose.

REFERENCES

Aiken, R.B. Orla, https://outorah.org/p/47596/

Amerine M. A., W. Berg; and W. V. Cruess. Technology of Wine Making. 1972. Avi Publishing, Westport. Conn.

Amerine M. A., W. V. Cruess, H. W. Berg; R. E. Kunkee, C. S. Ough, V. L. Singleton, and A. D. Webb. Table Wines and Dessert and Appetizer Wines Technology of Winemaking 1967, Avi Publishing, Westport. Conn.

Amerine M. A. and M.A. Joslyn. Table Wines: The Technology of their Production. 1973. University of California Press, Berkeley.

Amerine M. A. and C. S. Ough, Wine and Must Analysis. 1974. John Wiley and Sons. Canada

Amerine, M.A. and E. B. Roessler Wines: Their Sensory Evaluation, 1983 (W.H. Freeman & Company).

Amerine, M.A. and V. L. Singleton. Wine, An Introduction. Revised edition 1975. University of California Press, Berkley.

Boulton, R.B., V.L. Singleton, L.F. Bisson, and R.E. Kunkee. Principles and Practices of Winemaking. 1996 Chapman & Hall (International Thomson Publishing). New York:

Crues, W.V., M.A. Joslyn, L.G. Sawell. Laboratory Examination of Wines and Other Fermented Fruit Products. 1934, Avi Publishing Co. New York.

Deuteronomy 22:9

Deuteronomy 22:10-11

Exodus 23:10-11

Frazier, N.W., J. P. Fulton, J.M. Thresh, R. H. Converse, E.H. Varney, and W. B. Hewitt. Virus Diseases of Small Fruits and Grapevines. 1970, University of California Press. Berkeley.

Goldberg, Rav Avraham Hillel, The Land and its Complete Mitzvot. 1983 Chish Productions, Bene Brak.

Irwin, J. Guide to Making Homemade Wine. 1992, Tiger Books International. London.

Johnson, H. Wine Companion 1987, Mitchell Beazley Intern. Ltd. London.

Johnson, H. Vintage: The Story of Wine. 198, Simon and Schuster. New York.

Johnson, H. and James Halliday. The Vintner's Art: How Great Wines are Made. 1992. Simon and Schuster. New York.

Kasimatis, A. N., B.E. Bearden, and K. Bowers. Wine Grape Varieties in the North Coast Counties of California. 1977 University of California Press. Berkeley.

Leviticus 19:19

Leviticus: 19:23-25

Leviticus: 23:14

Leviticus: 25: 6-7

Leviticus: 25:11

Leviticus: 25:22

Maimonides (Moshe Ben Maimon). *Mishne Torah*. 1180. Book 7. The Book of Agriculture, *Sefer Zeraim*. Treatise 5 on Second Tithe and Fourth Year's Fruit. *Ma'aser Shein V'Neta Reva'I*; Chapter 10, sec.9

Maimonides (Moshe Ben Maimon). *Mishne Torah*. 1180. Book 7. The Book of Agriculture, *Sefer Zeraim* Treatise 1 on Diverse Kinds, *Kilahyim* Chapter 1, sections 1-3.

Maimonides (Moshe Ben Maimon). *Mishne Torah*. 1180. Book7. The Book of Agriculture, *Sefer Zeraim* Treatise 1 on Diverse Kinds, *Kilahyim* Chapter 1, secs 4.

Maimonides (Moshe Ben Maimon). *Mishne Torah*. 1180. Book7. The Book of Agriculture, *Sefer Zeraim* Treatise 1 on Diverse Kinds, *Kilahyim* Chapter 1, secs 5.

Maimonides (Moshe Ben Maimon). *Mishne Torah*. 1180. Book7. The Book of Agriculture, *Sefer Zeraim* Treatise 1 on Diverse Kinds, *Kilahyim* Chapter 1, secs 7.

Maimonides (Moshe Ben Maimon). *Mishne Torah*. 1180. Book 5, The Book of Holiness, *Sefer Kedushah*; Treatise 2 on Forbidden Foods, *Ma'achalot Assurot*; Chapter 10, sec 8.

Maimonides (Moshe Ben Maimon). Mishne Torah. 1180. Book 5, The Book of Holiness, *Sefer Kedushah*; Treatise 2 on Forbidden Foods, *Ma'achalot Assurot*; Chapter 10, sec 11-12.

Maimonides (Moshe Ben Maimon). *Mishne Torah*. 1180. Book 5, The Book of Holiness, *Sefer Kedushah*; Treatise 2 on Forbidden Foods, *Ma'achalot Assurot*; Chapter 10, sec 21.

Margalit, Y. Winery Technology & Operations: a Handbook for Small Wineries. 1996: The Wine Appreciation Guild. San Francisco

Melamed, E. Pearls of Halacha, Brachot, Vol.3 Har Bracha Publications. Israel.

Montefiore, A. Wine Talk: Ancient wine. 2012. http://www.jpost.com/ Arts-and-Culture/Food-And-Wine/Wine-Talk-Ancient-wine

Muscatine, D., Amerine, M. A. Thompson, B., The Book of California Wine. 1984 University of California Press, Berkeley.

Olmo, H.P. 1948, Ruby Cabernet and Emerald Riesling. Calif. Agr. Exper. Stat. Bull. 704:1-12.

Ough, C.S. and M.A. Amerine 1967. Studies with controlled fermentation. X. Effect of fermentation temperature on some volatile compounds in wine. Am. J. Enology & Viticulture. 18: 157-164.

Peynaud, E. The Taste of Wine: The Art and Science of Wine Appreciation. 1987. Macdonald & Co. (Publishers) Ltd. London

Pretorius, I.S. 2000. Tailoring wine yeast for the new millennium: novel approaches to the ancient art of winemaking. http://onlinelibrary.wiley.com/doi/10.1002/1097-0061(20000615)16:8%3C675::AID-YEA585%   3E3.0.CO;2-B/full

Proverbs Chapter 23:20

Robinson, J. Vines, Grapes, Wines. 1986, Mitchell Beazley. London.

Robinson, J., (ed.) The Oxford Companion to Wine – third edition. 2006. Oxford University Press. Oxford

Sette, S. How to Store Wine Properly, and Why It Matters. 2024. https://www.wineenthusiast.com/basics/buying-and-collecting/how-to-store-wine/

Storm, J. An Introduction to Wines. 1955. Simon and Schuster. New York.

Webb, D.A, and H.W. Berg, Terms used in tasting. 1955. Wines and Vines (36 (7) 25-28.

Wein, B. Wine, http://www.rabbiwein.com/

blog/wine-529.html

ABOUT THE AUTHOR

Dr. Barry Nadel was born in Texas (July 11, 1953) and grew up in San Jose, California (before it was Silicon Valley), in a traditional home that was Shomer Shabbat and kashrut. From 1971 to 1973, he studied Archaeology and Anthropology and switched to Enology and Viticulture, receiving his B.Sc. from UC Davis (1975) and his M.Sc. in grape genetics in 1977. In 1976, he won the Winkler Scholarship from the Department of Viticulture and Enology.

That same summer, he made aliyah to Israel to do his PhD in plant genetics at the Faculty of Agriculture, Hebrew University in Rehovot, which he received in 1981.

Dr. Nadel was for six years plant biotechnology and physiology researcher at the Faculty of Agriculture. He then founded his own small vegetable seed company and ran it for 22 years, responsible for plant breeding, stock seed maintenance, and seed production.

He served in the Army reserves for 13 years in the artillery. Later, he was a full-time volunteer for the Border Police, responsible for the security of Moshav Kfar Pines for ten years.

Dr. Nadel has three daughters, one son, and eleven grandchildren (five girls and six boys). He is divorced and a widower. He has been writing for over 40 years both scientific and non-fiction works. For the past 35 years, Dr. Nadel has been writing fiction. In 2013, he decided to publish a fiction project called the Hoshiyan Chronicles. It is a highly spiritual work based on the principles of justice, Righteousness, and Faith (www.drbnadel.com).

Books by Dr. Barry Nadel

Novels: The Hoshiyan Chronicles

Seeking the Light of Justice

Saving the Light of Justice

Oath of Peace

Forging the light of Justice

Prophecy of the Light of Justice

National Intelligence Agency

Farmer, Scholar, Prince

Mysterious Birth of the Light of Justice

Forging of a Spiritual Warrior

Forged in Fire

The Light of Justice: Evolution of Leadership

Spiritual Spy

Brewing Storm

Worthy of Love

Ultimate Treason

Enthroned in Sorrow

Warriors of Defiance

Justice Amidst Adversity

Virtue Among Depravity

Coming soon The Martyred Queen

Home Wine Making

The Art of Kosher Wine Making

Secrets of Home Wine Making

Organic Greenhouse Production

Greenhouse Setup Manual

Spice and Herb Production in Greenhouses

Vegetable Production in Greenhouses

The Production of Medicinal Cannabis in Greenhouses

All books are Available on Amazon.